We Celebrate the Eucharist

Guidelines for
Parents and Catechists

We Cel
the Eu

We Celebrate the Eucharist

Guidelines for
Parents and Catechists

Christiane Brusselmans • Brian A. Haggerty

Silver Burdett Company   Morristown, N.J. • Glenview, Ill. • Palo Alto • Dallas • Atlanta

Acknowledgments

Excerpts from *The New American Bible*

© Confraternity of Christian Doctrine, 1970, are used

by permission of copyright owner.

English translation of excerpts from the *Roman

Missal.* Copyright © 1973, International Committee

on English in the Liturgy, Inc. All rights reserved.

Pages 1-2: Excerpt from *A New Catechism: Catholic

Faith for Adults,* pp. 333-334. Copyright © 1967

and 1969 Herder and Herder. Used by permission

of The Seabury Press and Search Press.

Page 3: English translation of excerpt from the

Directory for Masses with Children.

Copyright © 1973, International Committee on

English in the Liturgy, Inc. All rights reserved.

Page 14: Excerpt from *Instruction on Eucharistic

Worship,* par. 14, published by the United States

Catholic Conference.

Page 35: Excerpt from "Celebration: A Human

Need" by Margaret Mead from *the catechist,* March

1968, pp. 8-9. © 1968 by George A. Pflaum,

Publisher, a division of Standard International

Corporation. Reprinted by permission of Peter Li, Inc.

Picture Credits

Burk Uzzle for Silver Burdett.

Contents

Introduction *vi*

1. The Eucharist: It's About Belonging *22*
   Group Session 25   Home Session 30

2. The Eucharist: It's About Celebrating *34*
   Group Session 38   Home Session 41

3. The Eucharist: It's About Making Peace *44*
   Group Session 47   Home Session 50

4. The Eucharist: It's About Listening *54*
   Group Session 58   Home Session 62

5. The Eucharist: It's About Caring *66*
   Group Session 69   Home Session 73

6. The Eucharist: It's About Giving Thanks for Creation *76*
   Group Session 80   Home Session 83

7. The Eucharist: It's About Giving Thanks for New Life *86*
   Group Session 89   Home Session 92

8. The Eucharist: It's About Sharing a Meal *96*
   Group Session 99   Home Session 102

9. The Eucharist: It's About Going Forth
   to Make a Better World *106*
   Group Session 110   Home Session 113

Introduction

WE CELEBRATE THE EUCHARIST is a program of "integrated catechesis." What does this mean?

It means that our program integrates both *persons* and *purposes*. First, it involves not only the children preparing for First Communion, but also their families, their teachers, their clergy, and their whole Christian community, or parish. Second, it means that we shall be preparing the children not just for First Communion, but for the Christian life itself, which is a eucharistic life. We shall all be preparing for the children's First Communion, and for their and our own life of love and service for God and neighbor, with the Eucharist at its center.

At the heart of the liturgical changes that have taken place in the Church is a renewal of eucharistic theology. The Mass, the Eucharist, is the Lord's sacrificial meal. Here his great deed of love for us—his death and resurrection—becomes really present to us for our salvation.

The Church's renewed interest in the depths and implications of this ancient reality has had a great effect on how children are introduced to it.

The Eucharist, proclaims Vatican II, is the affair of a community, a people, the people of God. It cannot be the affair of an individual merely. A child's reception of Holy Communion for the first time is, in a way, the deed of a whole people, the Christian people. More especially, it is the deed of the child's local Christian community, the parish—especially the child's parents and teachers.

The Mass and the Life of the Church Moreover, today's eucharistic theology emphasizes that the Mass is not just something to take time out for once a week—merely a different, more sacred activity. The Eucharist is something much deeper and more important than that. It is a center, a focal point, where Christians come together for love of their Lord, who is present to them, and then go out from it again like radii of a circle

A child's sacramental initiation is a responsibility to be shared —

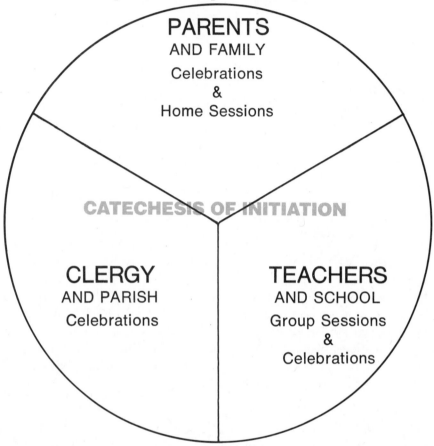

PARENTS
AND FAMILY
Celebrations
&
Home Sessions

CATECHESIS OF INITIATION

CLERGY
AND PARISH
Celebrations

TEACHERS
AND SCHOOL
Group Sessions
&
Celebrations

to make their Lord, who has become still more present to them now, present as well to the world.

In the spirit of the eucharistic renewal, We Celebrate the Eucharist has been prepared to initiate children, parents, teachers, and parish into the eucharistic life of faith and service that the children's First Communion implies. This is what we mean when we say our program is one of "integrated catechesis."

The Meaning of the Eucharist   The attitude and spirit that we hope shine through in every stage of our program of eucharistic initiation are expressed in *A New Catechism: Catholic Faith for Adults.*

The Eucharist has often been pondered, discussed and written about. And new light can still be thrown on it in each age. It is the focus of all the great realities of faith. Hence it is not surprising that in each period of Church history new facets and values are revealed in this so divinely simple gesture. At one time Christians stress their unity.

At other times, thanksgiving to the Father. Then again, the sacrifice. Or Jesus' presence. And there must still be treasures as yet undiscovered within the mystery. Jesus is always new in his greatest mystery.

In the Eucharist we are confronted with an inexhaustible mystery. It is this realization that lies at the heart of WE CELEBRATE THE EUCHARIST.

The Eucharist is a mystery, not a problem. A problem is something to be solved. A mystery is not something to be solved, but something to be entered into. In the past, we sometimes treated the Eucharist as a problem. We analyzed it, scrutinized it, tried to "explain" how Jesus could be in the host, or be the host, without always attending very carefully to the Christian importance of having him with us so intimately. We were sometimes distracted by problem-solving. But the Eucharist is not a problem. It is a mystery. It is like a bottomless well. No matter how much refreshment we draw from it, there is always as much left as before we began.

As a mystery, the Eucharist is something to be experienced, entered into. This is why the *Instruction on Eucharistic Worship* directs us to dwell on the "principal rites and prayers" of the Mass. Through the words and symbols of the liturgy, we will *live* the Eucharist, both in church and outside. We will live it as a mystery—as one deep, urgent, and joyful experience after another. It's about belonging, celebrating, making peace, listening, and caring. We will live it as a meal we share with others, as a sacrifice of love, as a funeral memorial of our great friend who died and rose again, and as a thrilling command to go out and prepare a better world. We are not simply preparing children for a First Communion ceremony. We are preparing them for the whole Christian life, the eucharistic life of a people who celebrate together at the Lord's altar, hear his word and eat his flesh, and then, filled with his new life, go out to ready the world for his return. We are preparing children not just for a First Communion ceremony, but for "full incorporation into the body of Christ."

Rome's *Directory for Masses with Children* recommends that a eucharistic catechesis be built on human values and experiences.

These values are the activity of the community, exchange of greetings, capacity to listen and grant pardon, expression of gratitude, experience of symbolic actions, a meal of friendship, and festive celebration (No. 9).

Nine Themes WE CELEBRATE THE EUCHARIST follows this directive. It centers on nine themes of human and Christian living. Each theme begins with some experience and activity that is of special importance simply for *living*—sharing a meal, for example. Then this experience is deepened by reflection, revealing its Christian dimension—its importance for *Christian living.*

The Mystery of the Eucharist

	Elements of the Eucharist	Themes of the Eucharist
1	Baptism	Belonging
2	Procession, Song, Greeting, Prayer	Celebrating
3	Penitential Rite, Our Father, Rite of Peace	Making Peace
4	Liturgy of the Word	Listening
5	Prayer of the Faithful	Caring
6	Preparation and Presentation of the Gifts; Preface; Holy, Holy, Holy	Giving Thanks for Creation
7	Eucharistic Prayer	Giving Thanks for New Life
8	Rite of Communion	Sharing a Meal
9	Rite of Dismissal	Going Forth to Make a Better World

Each theme, after the first, corresponds to a part of the eucharistic liturgy.

Each of the nine themes is introduced to the children in groups, deepened in a celebration in church, and finally assimilated more deeply at home.

The Eucharist Is About Belonging The gathering of Christians around the table of their Lord presupposes a unity, a community, already existing. The Eucharist is the gathering of those who have been baptized in Christ, and so belong to him. They have already entered together into his saving new life. Now they join again at his holy table to be nourished anew by the source of their Christ-life, the saving love of God.

The Eucharist Is About Celebrating The baptismal community wishes to proclaim with one voice who they are and who they are called to be. The opening prayers and songs of their celebration begin to draw them together on the Lord's day in the presence of the risen Jesus. "Where two or three are gathered in my name, there am I in their midst" (Matthew 18:20). Jesus is present to us through the celebrant and in the Christian community. Indeed it is his active presence that gives rise to the celebration in the first place.

The Eucharist Is About Making Peace The Eucharist is to be a celebration of Christian oneness. Christians must therefore be willing to tear down the walls of sinfulness that separate them from one another. The Penitential Rite, the Our Father, the Sign of Peace, express their desire to forgive and their need to be forgiven.

The Eucharist Is About Listening The Eucharist is the ultimate gesture of God's life-saving love for us. The Word, in either Testament, proclaims that love, and so "explains" that gesture to our minds and hearts. Jesus is really present to us in the Word his Church proclaims.

The Eucharist Is About Caring We respond to Jesus' word of love and concern for us. We voice our own concern and care for others in the Prayer of the Faithful. This expression in word of our dynamic concern means we intend to care for others in deed as well.

The Eucharist Is About Giving Thanks for Creation In the Preparation of the Gifts and the Eucharistic Prayer, we offer thanks in word and gesture for all the gifts God has given us. By carrying bread and wine to him we thank him for this world, the people in it, and all the other signs of his love that surround us.

The Eucharist Is About Giving Thanks for New Life We continue to thank God for his love, shown most of all in the gifts that have given us new life. The Incarnation and death and resurrection of Jesus are the greatest of these. The Eucharist recalls these events to us actively and anew. In the Eucharistic Prayer we thank God for them and for the new life they have brought us. We recall the saving sacrifice of Jesus, which gave us our rebirth. In the real presence of the risen Lord, and moved by his Spirit, we proclaim our faith in the "wonderful works of God" by which he saves us.

The Eucharist Is About Sharing a Meal Now that we have thanked God for his gifts of creation, we share in them. Bread and wine nourish God's people bodily. Now by his power they are transformed to provide spiritual nourishment. In these sacred elements we genuinely partake of the risen Lord, receive him as our food, for he is really and entirely present in them, risen and alive. By assimilating one and the same Jesus as our food, we all become, in him, one body together—the Church.

The Eucharist Is About Going Forth to Make a Better World Strengthened with the Lord received in the word, in the bread, and in our sisters and brothers, we are sent out into the world. Sustained by God's love, we go forth with a mission: to work toward that world that responds to his love.

Thus many themes emerge from our experience of the Eucharist. The Eucharist is about all of them. It's about belonging, celebrating, making peace, listening, caring, giving thanks for creation and for new life, sharing a meal, and going forth to make a better world. It's about many things we do and say. But always it's about what God has done for us. A program of initiation into the Eucharist should try to take account both of what we are doing and saying, and of what God has done and said, what he is doing and saying. We have tried to do this.

Hence WE CELEBRATE THE EUCHARIST will by no means be just a "preparation for First Holy Communion." It will be a preparation for the whole experience of the Eucharist—including, as the crown of that experience, our going forth from the eucharistic assembly to live a truly Christian life—to make the world better by our faith and our works.

Organization of the Program

How does God usually enter into a relationship with a believer? In Old and New Testaments alike, the prophets and Jesus begin with daily life as their starting point. "One day a farmer went out sowing. Part of what he sowed landed on a footpath," Jesus begins (Matthew 13:4). Or "No one lights a lamp and puts it under a bushel basket" (Luke 8:16). God uses our human experiences to lead us to understand his love for us. In fact, these experiences are often the very occasions of his pouring forth that love on us.

We ourselves can hardly do better. WE CELEBRATE THE EUCHARIST is based on human experience. Each of its nine themes begins by inviting the children to consider some fundamental human experience of their daily lives—celebrating, for instance, or listening, or sharing a meal. Thus our approach tries to be faithful to the way God himself teaches us his love.

This approach is also faithful to the psychology of young children. Seven- and eight-year-olds live in the present moment. And they tend to think of the world as revolving around themselves. Hence we suggest activities that call upon the child simply to reflect, at first, on his or her own life experiences. Then we develop the theme, to disclose its full Christian dimension.

The Four Sessions Each of the nine themes in our program is presented in four different meetings, or sessions—one for the parents and catechists, one for the children, one for everyone, and one at home.

WHAT?	FOR WHOM?	WHERE?	BY WHOM?
1. **ADULT SESSION**	Parents, catechists	School, or elsewhere	Program director, or other qualified person
2. **GROUP SESSION**	Children	School, or elsewhere	Catechists
3. **CELEBRATION**	Children, parents, catechists, perhaps parish	Church or chapel	Priest, or other leader
4. **HOME SESSION**	Family	Home	Parents

Let us take the first theme—Belonging—and see what happens in each of the four sessions. The *first session* is for the parents and the catechists of the children being initiated into the Eucharist. The program director, or someone else well qualified, introduces the theme. In the first adult meeting, the theme will be Belonging—belonging in a simply human way to our families, our groups, but also belonging to the family of God, the Church, by baptism. The instructor will try to give the parents and teachers a real taste of this theme, not just an abstract explanation.

The person who conducts this session will not only present the theme, but will also make suggestions on how to guide the children in the theme. He or she will explain how to use this book, *Guidelines for Parents and Catechists,* how the theme relates to the other themes, and so on. Catechists and parents will gain the information, guidance, and confidence they need to fulfill their roles as teachers of their children.

The *second session* is a period of instruction for the children. It will usually be held at school, either in the parochial school or at CCD. But it might, according to circumstances, be held in someone's home in the neighborhood. *This session is called the group session in this book.* Here the children are invited to reflect on their experience of belonging—belonging to their family at home, for instance. Then they begin to consider another, even better, belonging—belonging to the family of God.

The *third session* is a liturgical celebration. It may be the Eucharist, or it may be a non-eucharistic celebration. Children, parents, catechists, perhaps even the parish as the children's Christian community, are invited to this celebration. Here the sacred dimension of belonging—belonging to the family of God—is deepened by the experience of praying and celebrating together.

The *fourth session* is the home session. Essentially, it is an informal meeting between parents and child, in which the theme of belonging—to the family at home and then to the family of God—is broadened and deepened. The child has the opportunity to assimilate the word of God proclaimed in the celebration and to integrate it more fully into his or her daily life.

Now let us look at the latter three of these four sessions in greater detail.

The Group Session By group session we mean the second session on each theme, the instructional meeting for the children conducted by the catechists. It is held at school or in someone's home in the neighborhood. Here the new theme is introduced to the children who are being initiated into the Eucharist.

First, catechists or catechist-aides meet with the children in groups of half a dozen or so. They welcome each child to the group and establish an atmosphere of friendliness and mutual confidence. A spirit of community pervades the whole session.

Second, the child's homework is reviewed. It should take only ten minutes or so for the children to share with their catechist or aide and with one another what they have done at home on the preceding theme.

Third, the new theme is introduced. This presentation may be made by one principal catechist. In this case the smaller groups will join together for this part of the session. Often the principal catechist will be the director or coordinator. In any case he or she will be an experienced teacher, well-versed in the psychology of the young child. This large-group format is particularly advisable where the small-group catechists are inexperienced and can learn by observing an experienced teacher.

Whether the presentation of the theme is made in the small groups or in one large group, it will be based on experiences familiar to the children, and with as much involvement as possible on their part. The experiences will be drawn from everyday life. They may be taken from the family environment, from the relationships between children and parents, brothers and sisters. A number of these experiences are suggested in this book, theme by theme. But since the children's horizon, by the time they are seven or eight years old, is beginning to expand beyond the home, the catechist or catechist-aide will also make use of experiences in school and neighborhood, and even on television. The experiences suggested in this book cannot accommodate all situations. The catechist must be ready to modify and adapt as needed. The presentation of the theme should take about twenty minutes.

Fourth, the new theme is assimilated in the small groups. Now the catechists or catechist-aides help the children assimilate the theme through activities like drawing, writing, reading, discussion, and prayer. The children should progress at their own pace, benefiting from frequent individual contact with the mature person in charge of the small group. The activities suggested in this book require about twenty-five minutes for this fourth step in the group session.

The children may then be dismissed. There is no need to gather them for a general meeting at this point unless the third session, the celebration, is scheduled to take place now. In this case a fifteen-minute recess should be allowed.

The work of the catechists and catechist-aides is of capital importance. It demands preparation. Even if it is not they who are to make the presentation of the new theme, they must prepare it, since the fourth step (the assimilation of the new theme in small groups) flows from it immediately and naturally. Every catechist and catechist-aide should have a copy of this book, *Guidelines*, as well as a copy of the child's book, the "golden book," in order to prepare the group session adequately.

9

The Celebration The session that follows the children's, or group, session is devoted entirely to community prayer. It is a liturgical celebration, either a eucharistic one or a non-eucharistic one. It may be a Saturday evening or Sunday Mass. Or it may be scheduled on a weekday, and not be a Mass, and thus be better geared to the stage of eucharistic initiation in which the young children find themselves at the moment. In the celebrations God's revelation is presented to the children in a setting of Christian community, and in the concrete and universal language of liturgy. The human experience of every day is transformed, carried one giant step further, into the dimension of the sacred. For example, in the first celebration, children who belong to families now celebrate their belonging to the family of God.

The great advantage of this liturgical experience is the benefit to the children of the witness and the faith of adults with whom they closely identify. The presence of parents and catechists is essential. So too is their active external and interior participation. Children's faith grows by being nourished by the faith of the adults around them. A habit of externally and interiorly devout participation at liturgy will be formed.

The Home Session The liturgical experience of the celebration serves as a base for the fourth and last session on each theme, the home session. The catechesis at home offers the child the opportunity of assimilating the word of God even more fully by integrating it into his or her daily life. The daily experiences of the child, enlightened by the word of God in the celebration, are now deepened at home. Together with his or her parents, the child reflects on the relationship between the word of God and everyday life. The experiences and activities of daily life are the occasions of an outpouring of the love of God and the work of the Holy Spirit. Thus these experiences are true occasions of God's revelation. More than anyone else, parents can enlighten the life of their child by forming the habit of pointing out to him or her, often, how God is entering the child's life in this way or that—even in the most ordinary circumstances of daily living.

To assist parents in carrying out their responsibility in the home sessions, this book contains a theological reflection for parents on each theme, along with procedures and activities that can help them deepen the theme with their children. Besides the help this book can give, the adult session (the first session) on each theme will provide further preparation. Parents and catechists will have the occasion there to deepen their own faith by reflection, study, and discussion.

The Atmosphere The first thing one senses upon entering a place where learning is supposed to be happening is the atmosphere. The atmosphere can either support or impair the development that should be going on. Children cannot be properly attentive, active, or even happy if they are forced to try to engage in learning in a disordered space, or if their teacher is distracted by other occupations or is inadequately prepared. True growth can take place only where a teacher or a parent brings to an attractive and peaceful setting ideas that are planned to respond to a young child's need for security and creativity.

In the group session the catechist or catechist-aide must know in advance what activities are going to be performed. At the same time he or she must be ready to sincerely respect the personal views and wishes of the children. Thus while assigning the work to be done, the catechist must neither do the children's work for them nor burden them with too many activities. A child will feel more fulfilled after having done a few things successfully than after rushing through a great many different things. For this reason, not all the activities we recommend need be done by all the children. Make a first selection yourself, then perhaps offer the children a choice.

The atmosphere of the group session also requires that the children realize their activities are not going to be "graded"—evaluated on the same basis as other school activities. The group session is a time for reflection and discussion about the personal experiences of life. At no time should a spirit of competition be allowed to prevail. Each child should be allowed to work at his or her own pace and in his or her own way. The work should be done in a family spirit, and the result offered to God, who sees its real, not its superficial, value.

In the home session, too, the atmosphere should be one of friendly and confident familiarity. Nevertheless the home session should be prepared and conducted carefully and seriously. The child should sense that parents are devoting this time to him or her alone. The place for the session, too, should be chosen carefully. Care should be taken to avoid constant interruptions.

The home session is the time for reflection on the celebration—the liturgical experience of the theme. This can be a very pleasant, intimate recollection of the experience. The parent is first of all a parent, who loves his or her children. He or she is also a teacher, who has received a divine commission to give witness to the faith before the child and to enlighten the child by the word of God. The activities parent and child perform together can be the loving and fruitful prolongation of the spirit of the celebration.

A home session need not be confined to one sitting. Circumstances will determine whether it consists of one meeting or several. But the time, or times, should be set aside in advance—not only to get the job done efficiently, but also as a sign of the importance of the task and the **serious** interest of the parents.

When parents are asked to substitute for neighborhood parents who are not available for a home session, they should work with the children of those parents just as they do with their own children. They should strive for a relationship of collaboration and friendship with the children, as well as with their parents.

The Child's Book Perhaps the most concrete symbol of the child's eucharistic preparation, throughout the program, will be the "golden book," the child's book. It is divided equally into nine sections, corresponding to the nine themes of our program. Each section is then divided as follows:

1. Two pages of photographs, representing some aspect of the human experience of the theme

2. Two pages of text—a reflection on the human experience depicted, calling for a response

3. Two pages emphasizing the liturgical experience of the theme

4. Two pages presenting a biblical experience, together with activities for deepening the Christian dimension of the experience

Suggestions on how to use these pages in the group and the home sessions are presented in the present book.

Methodology in Religious Education

Seven- and eight-year-old children learn by doing. They assimilate ideas and develop attitudes actively. They need reading, drawing, gestures, writing, and song, as well as dialogue and reflection.

WE CELEBRATE THE EUCHARIST tries to help the children become aware of, and further reflect on, their own human experiences and those of their community, in order to perceive the Christian dimension of these experiences. This will be their best preparation for the Christian life, the eucharistic life. We aim at Christian conviction, attitudes, and commitment. In striving to accomplish this end we shall adapt ourselves to the way young children learn: We shall invite them to perform activities.

The activities we suggest are calculated to open the children to deeper awareness. We try to help them become more capable of personal responses to God's love. Hence these activities should be carried out in a spirit of spontaneous and sincere self-expression. They are aimed at the total person. Children discover God not with their minds alone, but with their whole being, and they respond to his call with their whole being. Their senses, intelligence, will, and memory come into play spontaneously and together in their experiences of every day. That is why we suggest diverse, well-planned activities that engage the whole person, not the mind alone or the motor faculty alone. We want to encourage free expression of ideas and to respect individual personalities.

A list of guidelines might be helpful. To help children discover God in their daily lives and respond to him in a personal way, we suggest the following:

⚙ Try to understand what the child wants to express.

⚙ Avoid imposing your own opinion or viewpoint.

⚙ Avoid looking for visible, measurable "success."

⚙ Avoid dictating answrs. Bear witness to your own Christian convictions, attitudes, commitments. This is not dictating answers. Faith is a gift—not only in the sowing, but also in the increase.

WE CELEBRATE THE EUCHARIST follows an approach that is geared to the way young children learn. We begin with the experiences and activities of the children's everyday life: belonging, celebrating, forgiving and being forgiven, listening, caring, giving thanks, sharing a meal, going out to do something creative. From these experiences as starting points, our program gradually leads the children into the main experiences of the Eucharist. And their families and teachers come along, leading them, following them, until all together have been initiated more deeply into this great mystery of our faith. Our children will have assimilated the Eucharist as something in their daily lives—not something just like anything else, of course, but its very center. Parents and catechists will have deepened and personalized their experience of the Eucharist.

The Sacred Congregation of Rites, in its May 1967 *Instruction on Eucharistic Worship,* directed eucharistic catechists to emphasize the Mass and the place of the Mass in the life of the Church.

Those who have charge of the religious instruction of children, especially parents, parish priests, and teachers, should be careful when they are introducing them gradually to the mystery of salvation, to give emphasis to instruction on the Mass. Instruction about the Eucharist, while being suited to the age and abilities of children, should aim to convey the meaning of the Mass through the principal rites and prayers. It should also explain the place of the Mass in participation in the life of the Church. All this should be borne in mind especially when children are being prepared for First Communion so that First Communion may be seen as the full incorporation into the body of Christ (No. 14).

Parents are Teachers   Parents are listed first for a reason. The Church has long taught that parents are the first teachers of their children. They are first not only in order of time, but also in order of importance. Where faith is concerned, this is even truer than for other kinds of learning. Faith is not just an activity or a quality of the mind. It is an activity and a quality of the whole person. It is acquired by personal contact with a person of faith. And it grows by that same contact, as well as being practiced. For a child born into the "household of the faith," by far the most important persons of faith are his or her parents.

Activities for the Program

Prayer Prayer is any raising of the mind and heart to God. Prayer does not have to be in words. Any reflection on life in the light of God's revelation, is prayer. But there should be moments of explicit prayer, when we consciously address God. And there should be moments of communal prayer, when we address God together. Here are some guidelines for the prayer leader—the parent or teacher who is about to pray with his or her children.

- ☼ Wait until the children are perfectly quiet. Help them become aware that they are in God's presence and that it is to God they are addressing themselves.

- ☼ Do not try to make the children pray. Pray with them. Give them the example of an external attitude that shows a prayerful interior attitude.

- ☼ Pray often by singing. Song is an excellent vehicle for the prayer of the mind, of the heart, even of the body (in gestures), all at once. We respond to God's love with our whole person.

Since the home sessions are intimate dialogues between parents and child, prayer here will be even more spontaneous than in the schoolroom or the church. The session outlines in this book give suggestions for prayers parents may use in concluding the work done together with their child. Parents should also pray with their child by singing the songs that were taught during the class sessions and used during the celebrations. The songs on the record *We Celebrate the Eucharist* have been written with this purpose in mind.

15

It is in the celebrations, of course, that prayer takes on its most important communal form. One of the purposes of WE CELEBRATE THE EUCHARIST is to initiate the child into the prayers and songs of the Christian community gathered in the celebration of the Eucharist.

We ask parents to review with their children the liturgical prayers and dialogues of the Eucharist. These are part of our Christian community worship. It will be good practice to repeat these prayers and dialogues from time to time between sessions, so that the children become thoroughly familiar with them. *The Lord be with you—And also with you* is an example. A Mass book or missalette will contain them, and the child's book, the "golden book," excerpts a number of them in smaller type.

Singing Singing can be an individual or a communal activity. We make use of song in our program to provide young children and the adults closest to them with a means of expressing a spiritual attitude, and as an aid in preparing them to join the liturgical singing of the Christian community. Sometimes the words of a song we recommend may be partially beyond the comprehension of the children. (This will not be true of the record *We Celebrate in Eucharist.*) This is because we feel it is important to help children join their voices early in the adult songs of the Christian community. The program director and the catechists will choose the songs to be learned for the celebrations, at which children and adults will be singing the same songs together.

To teach a song, the catechist may use the following procedure. First, show the children the words in large print on a poster or on the chalkboard. Then ask them to just listen as you sing the song or play a recording of it. Explain the words and their meaning—in dialogue with the children if possible. Now sing just one phrase of the song. Ask the children to hum along as you repeat the phrase. Then have them sing the phrase with you. Follow the same method for the rest of the song, phrase by phrase. Finally, bind the whole song together.

Gestures to accompany the song will often help give it its full meaning, as well as help maintain the rhythm and tempo. With a little repetition the text will be memorized, and the song can be a prayer.

From time to time, review with the children the songs they have learned. As the program progresses, the children will have expanded their repertoire and their ability to enhance the celebrations with song. In the home sessions, the songs the children have learned will be an excellent vehicle for prayer, as well as for reviewing themes. A considerable help here would be a home copy of the record *We Celebrate the Eucharist*—unless it is preferred to present the record later as a surprise First Communion gift. Other albums, too, can be used at home. Your catechist will be glad to let you know which albums and which songs in the albums have been used in your child's eucharistic catechesis.

Gestures The language of gesture is a universal one. Gestures express not only ideas, but inner attitudes and feelings as well. This is one reason why gestures are particularly appropriate for prayer or song. Hence it is important to acquaint children early with the gestures of the liturgy. When children are impressed with the way in which an adult has expressed an attitude by means of a gesture, they like to imitate that gesture. In so doing, they assimilate something of the adult's inner attitude. Hence the gestures of the liturgy are particularly apt for discussion and practice. The children can learn to imitate them and, in so doing, will internalize the attitude they express. The priest's gesture of greeting while saying "The Lord be with you" is an example. But so are the congregation's gestures—standing attentively, sitting reverently, kneeling humbly, exchanging the greeting of peace.

Group Discussion To enable all the children to express themselves adequately, and to create an atmosphere conducive to discovery, dialogue and discussion should be conducted in large as well as small groups. Seven- and eight-year-olds react spontaneously to what they see, think, feel, and do. They are often very responsive to the question/discussion approach.

Here are some hints for leading a discussion:

- ❁ Ask a question of the whole group. After a moment's pause, call on an individual for an answer. First calling on the child and then asking the question will invite the rest of the group to "tune out."

- ❁ Insist the children wait to be called on. Do not allow them all to answer at once.

- ❁ Give every child the opportunity to participate.

17

⚙ Learn to ask clear, precise questions. A child who does not understand what you are asking will risk answering incorrectly, and may then feel frustrated and ashamed. The next time, he or she may refuse to answer. A child who answers correctly will want to try again.

⚙ Avoid simple Yes or No questions.

⚙ Do not ask "conformity questions," such as "Do you love Jesus? Are you always kind to your brothers and sisters?" The children will answer what they think they ought to answer, rather than what is true.

⚙ Never ridicule. If a child answers incorrectly, use some correct (or less incorrect) element in the answer and try to draw out a better answer as in the following example. A single mocking or sarcastic remark can do irreparable damage.

Catechist: "Belonging. What are some other groups we can belong to? [Pause] Jimmy."

Jimmy [not understanding]: "A zoo." [Class laughter]
Catechist: "Well, we often go to the zoo *in* a group, don't we? In a group we belong to. Who might go to the zoo *with* you? [Pause] Jimmy."

Jimmy: "My brother." [Or "Kids."]

Catechist: "That's right, Jimmy, our brothers and sisters—our family." [Or "Our classmates—our class in school."] "Very good! Did the rest of you hear Jimmy's answer? We belong to our family." [Or "We belong to our class in school."]

Of course, where a group of children are less equipped to express themselves verbally, the proportion of activities based on discussion should be reduced. Motor-oriented activities—making things, drawing, drama or pantomime—should replace some of them.

Reading and Memorization The best material for a reading exercise will often be found in the child's book, the "golden book." It will provide summaries of the themes to read, prayers to read or pray or memorize, and many adapted biblical texts.

Writing The writing activities in the child's book are not intended as exercises in spelling or penmanship. Parents or teachers may be tempted to look for fine writing. This would be a mistake. Our program of eucharistic initiation aims at eucharistic living, where academic perfection does not enjoy first priority. Of first priority is a grasp, with mind and heart, of the Christian faith—a eucharistic faith that overflows into good works. It is important, however, that children show their respect for the importance of their work by the *effort* of their best writing and best spelling, their best drawing, and so forth. And they should be able to count on the assistance of an adult who will help them understand exactly what is asked of them, help them spell words correctly, and the like. It is important for the children to be able to show their golden book proudly and happily to parents, teachers, and all who are interested in their First Communion.

Drawing A glance into the child's book will show that drawing is suggested for each of the nine themes. Why do we use this activity so extensively?

Drawing is one of the best tools available for a pedagogy of the whole person. In their drawings children reveal themselves to others and to themselves. And they reveal their total selves, not just their ideas. They show not only what is on their mind, but also what is in their heart. They reveal what they have grasped and what they have not grasped, on both the intellectual and the emotional levels. They express their loves and dislikes, their needs, their securities and insecurities, their strivings and desires. A child's drawing may seem to be intended to represent some external reality realistically, but it is actually meant to express the child's own internal world.

How often we hear a child say, "I don't know how to explain it, but I'll draw it for you." Or a child who is unable or unwilling to verbalize feelings of gratitude will make a drawing, and will come and say, "Here is a present I made for you"—all aglow interiorily, even if he or she is too reticent to smile. Especially in certain sociocultural milieus, where children may not verbalize as easily as the inexperienced teacher might expect them to, drawing can very well replace much discussion.

It is of the utmost importance for adults to realize that children and adults draw for different reasons. Young children are not very concerned about realism in art. Perspective, the "correct" use of color, and realistic contour, are just not important. Children use lines, shapes, and colors not to repeat on paper something that exists in outside reality—this would seem presumptuous and superfluous to them—but to put on paper their own reality within. They want to put on paper what *they* feel and know *about* reality. Unless adults realize this, they may mistake for poor drawing what is really an excellent re-presentation of the young artist's inner, perhaps very deep and intense, reality.

In WE CELEBRATE THE EUCHARIST, children use drawing to express their responses to human and religious experiences. What is important is not realism but inner grasp and fervor. As parents and catechists we should express our pleasure at the beauty of the inner grasp and fervor more than at the physically aesthetic perfections a child's drawing may have. Certainly we must be careful never to make fun of awkwardness or blunders—especially since the young artist may be expecting to be made fun of, as a product of unfortunate experience. What is important is that a drawing reveals something about the one who has made it.

The drawings suggested for each lesson are inspired by the theme of the lesson. The children should be free in their expression of the theme, but they should express the theme. Before beginning to draw, the children should be invited to reflect a little while.

> Teacher: "Let's show in a drawing what we have been thinking and telling about our family. First, let's close our eyes and see in our mind who belongs to our family. Let's think about our house, our father, our mother, our brothers and sisters. Now let's make a drawing of our home or our family. Let's do this drawing very well— with all our heart—so we can say 'Thank you' to God for belonging to a family."

Two conditions for the successful use of drawing in our program are ample space and good materials.

☼ Children need a large surface, with many pretty colors from which to choose. Felt-tipped pens are best. It is essential to use good materials.

☼ Children need ample work space. If they sit too close together, they will be distracted, and may begin to copy each other's ideas.

Interpretation of the Drawing The children's drawings will take on more meaning even for the children if they can show them to an adult and explain what they have done. When children show us their drawings, they are confiding to us their inner lives. We should welcome this and show respect for what they have presented in their drawings. We should help them express themselves further by asking a few specific questions. Then we can encourage the children to caption the drawing—to write a few words, perhaps a prayer, on the drawing to capture its meaning. A child who cannot do this can dictate the caption or prayer to an adult to write. Now we are involved in the child's interior life in a way most satisfying and beneficial to the child—and to us.

We should never treat a drawing as of no importance. We should therefore disapprove immediately of a drawing done hurriedly, or in a spirit of superficiality. A simple remark ought to suffice. "You can do better than this. Please do it over again." Or, "Please do it again—seriously, this time. You have all the time you need to do it well."

Not all children like to draw. Sometimes the reason is the child's experience of inadequate adult response. Adults may have discouraged a child from drawing by attempting to impose an adult realism. They may have tried to correct the child's perspective, contour, or color (thereby missing the whole point of the piece of art before them). Worse, they may have laughed at a drawing—ridiculed the child's awkwardness.

We must restore the child's confidence. Suggest a subject that is easy to depict and close to the child's experience—a house, for example. Give the child plenty of good materials and an ample area with enough privacy so that he or she will not be judged by a classmate, sibling, or adult. Show the child you have confidence in him or her. To the child who says, "I can't draw," answer calmly, "Maybe you can do it if I help you." If necessary, help by drawing a few lines yourself, just to get the child started. "You see, you can put your house there, and perhaps your mommy here. And who might go there?" As soon as the child begins to work, withdraw. If called, come back and help, as much as really necessary. Avoid giving the child rulers, erasers, and lead pencils.

Up to the age of ten, most children like to draw. After ten they tend to abandon it. If you have older children in this program you may wish to offer alternatives, such as collages, written narratives, mobiles, or the like. *21*

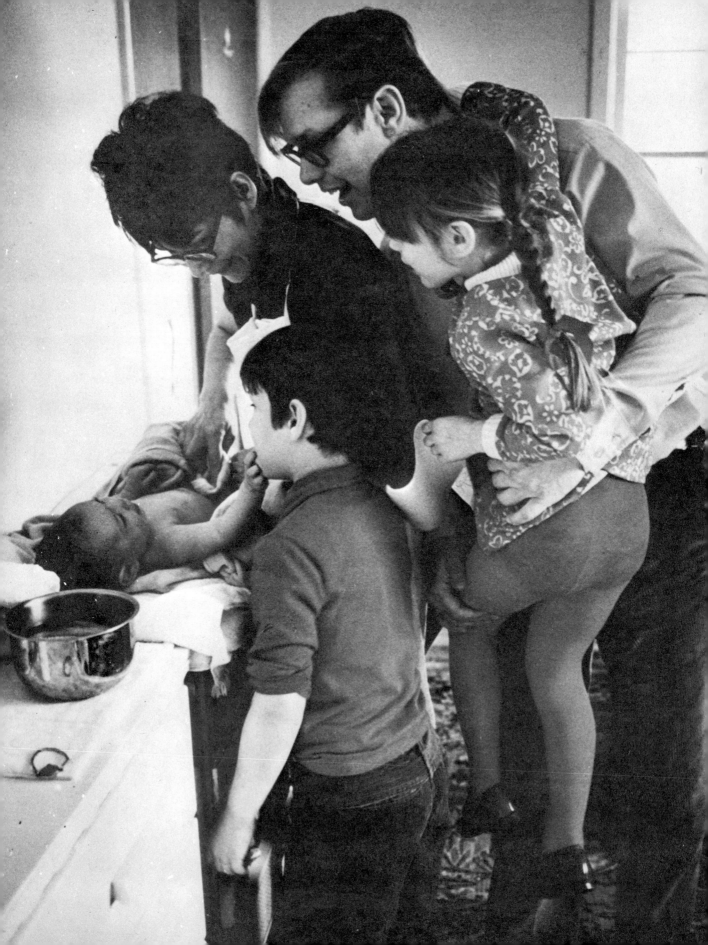

The Eucharist:

It's About Belonging

We are all *belongers*. We belong to a certain family, a certain nation, a certain ethnic group, a certain race. We may belong to the PTA, a bowling league, or a labor union.

Some groups we belong to because we were born into them. Others we chose because of their purpose.

One of the most profound and beautiful experiences of belonging that any of us can know is that of belonging to a family. It is undoubtedly the best experience we can have of the fact that people do belong together and that we do need others. Most of all, it is our first and most fundamental experience of a belonging that brings life itself.

Membership in a family does not depend first of all on us. It is not something we produce. Our entrance into our family is by birth, a result of the need two people have expressed for each other in the act of love. But it is only the beginning. The same love by which we began tc live nurtures us in our growth, giving life more and more. Sometimes the growth comes by startling changes. Sometimes it comes through apparent periods of slow, prolonged rest. But always, if there is openness and unselfishness on the part of those whose love gave life in the first place, new life can flower.

23

Belonging to a family is the human experience that most closely parallels the experience of being a Christian. In fact, we say we belong to "God's family, the Church."

We do not belong to the family of God because of anything we have done. We do not belong to it because we have a right to belong. Like our membership in our own families, our membership in the family of God is purely gratuitous. It is "for free." It is the result of an act of love by somebody else. The life-giving love of Jesus, made visible in the sacrament of baptism, incorporates us into his body, the family of God.

The body is one and has many members, but all the members, many though they are, are one body; and so it is with Christ. It was in one spirit that all of us ... were baptized into one body. ... You, then, are the body of Christ (1 Corinthians 12:12-13, 27).

And so we are born to life *with others,* in the family of God.

But as with our own family at home, birth is only a beginning. Our baptism is only the start. The love God showed us there continues to nurture us, and we grow—for example, through the Eucharist, a sign of the love that nourishes, and through penance, a sign of the love that restores. It is also given to us in the daily word and example of those who share Jesus' love with us. If the Christians around us are open and unselfish, our own Christian belonging can grow.

The gratuitousness of belonging to the family of God is certainly clear in the baptism of an infant. It is the baby's parents, who themselves received this gift once upon a time, who now present for baptism the product of their love. In the baptism of an adult, the convert—who already believes—*asks for faith* nevertheless. This is a striking sign that faith is a gift, something we receive, not something we produce. So is our belonging to the family of God.

The pouring of the life-giving waters of baptism symbolizes birth. It makes visible the life-giving that is happening—the life of new membership in the family of God.

The Christian community stands by, giving the witness of their faith. A baptism is a family affair, an affair of the family of God, just as much as our physical birth is an affair that intensely concerns our whole family at home. The priest or deacon, the parents and godparents, relatives and friends, and, more and more nowadays, other members of the parish, come to participate. This new life is a life *with others*. It is a *belonging*.

But birth—in this case, rebirth—is only a beginning. The anointing with oil, the bestowing of the white garment, the conferral of the lighted candle, all look to the future. These rites declare that not all is accomplished at baptism. They point to living as a member of Christ's body, as a member of his family. They underline the necessity of support from those with whom the newly baptized Christian shares Christian life and belonging. Baptism is but a beginning. Belonging to the family of God is both a gift and a task. Birth must be followed by growth.

In the early Church, these ceremonies were followed by a rite of initiation into the catechumenate. The catechumenate was the period of initiation into the Christian community. It took place in stages. When the catechumen—the newly baptized person—completed one stage, he or she was officially enrolled for the next stage of initiation. The final stage of the catechumenate was full participation in the Eucharist itself. We might consider the value of restoring this rite to our present celebration of Christian initiation.

WE CELEBRATE THE EUCHARIST is like the stages of the catechumenate. It presupposes baptism and culminates in full participation in the Eucharist. In the Church we become aware, through others, not only of our basic dependence on God for love that gives life, but of our need for the gift of growth, and of our task of sharing that growth with others. Our belonging to the family of God is just the beginning of an exchange of life and growth with our brothers and sisters in Christ all around us, in order that we *all* may "have life and have it to the full" (John 10:10).

Group Session

To help the children realize that through their parents they belong to a family in which they receive life and love

Aim

It is of the greatest importance that from the very beginning of this program the children experience their belonging to a human and Christian community. Therefore, take as much time as you need during this first meeting to get to know the children in a relaxed and friendly setting.

Welcome

25

Welcome each child with special love and joy. The child should be able to discover through your attitude that he or she belongs to a group of friends, and will meet regularly with them to prepare for the Eucharist.

I belong to a family.

Introduce yourself. Tell the children about yourself, your family, where you live, the kind of work you do, your hobbies, and your interests.

Write your name on a name tag and display it so that all the children may see it.

Discuss with the children what it means to be part of a family. Reflect with them on how good it is to return home and find people there to welcome us, to take care of us, to play with us, to love us.

State how important it is to share life, joy, and love with a family. Point out that through our parents we have received the gift of life. Our parents or foster parents have formed our family. Our parents or foster parents provide for our needs and give us a home.

If unhappy family situations exist for children in your group, you might adapt the presentation by asking the children to consider the many people in their community who truly care for them: foster parents, guardians, teachers, group leaders, kindly neighbors, interested adults. Help them recognize that these people care for them with interest, concern, and love.

You also belong to a family.

Ask the children to introduce themselves. Ask them to tell their first and last names, their brothers' and sisters' names. You might have them tell where they live, the name of the street, and the number of their house.

When all the children have introduced themselves, distribute brightly colored name tags and wax crayons or felt-tipped pens. Ask the children to print their first and last names on their name tag. Assist those children who need help. Then ask the children to pin their name tag to their clothing.

Presentation of the Communion Book

Distribute copies of the children's book. Encourage them to look through it for a few minutes. Comment on its beauty; then point out its main features. Tell the children that their book has many beautiful pictures. Ask them to look, for instance, at the first spread. Explain that they will read from their book and that there is space for them to write their thoughts, as on page 2. They will find words in their book taken from the Bible. Ask them to follow as you read page 6. These are adaptations of Isaiah 43 and Colossians 3. More space follows for drawing or for making a collage at home. Their book has many beautiful prayers they will use when they pray together.

Tell the children that their book will be part of their gift to Jesus on the day of their First Communion. They will offer their book to the Lord during the Offertory Procession. Ask them to take care of their book and to try to do good work in it.

Picture Discussion Ask the children to open their book to page 1. Give them time to look at the pictures. Help them reflect on the meaning of the experiences depicted there. You might initiate discussion of the positive values of belonging in the following manner. "Look at the children in the first picture. How can you tell that they are having fun? Do you think their teacher is having fun too? Tell us about a really good time you had with your teacher and your classmates." Conclude this picture discussion by pointing out that it is good to belong to a group of friends; it is good to belong to a teacher.

Activities

Ask the children to consider the second picture. You might ask, "What do you see in this picture? Who belongs to this family? Do you think this family is happy? How can you tell?" Summarize the children's responses by saying that it is good to belong to a family.

Reading Ask the children to turn to page 2. Have them read the text. If they need help, you might read the text to them or with them. As they go through the text, briefly indicate that they are to fill in the spaces provided.

Writing Give the children sufficient time and any assistance they may need to complete the sentences on page 2.

Drawing Invite the children to turn to page 3 and draw a picture of their family and perhaps their house. This activity should take about twenty minutes, but it is very important that each child be permitted to work at his or her own speed. Read carefully the instructions about drawing on pages 19–21 of this guide.

Interpretation As the children finish their drawings, speak privately with each one. Give them some guidelines to help them describe what

27

they are expressing. For example, "Tell me about your picture. Who is this? Who is that? What is her (his) name? Where are you?"

Writing   As you speak with each child, invite him or her to write down the name of each person in the picture. Spelling mistakes are acceptable at this age level. Assist only those children who ask you how to spell a word.

Singing   Teach Song 1 on the record *We Celebrate the Eucharist.* (See page 16, above, for suggestions on teaching a song.) You may wish to send home with each child a copy of the lyrics, so that the song may be used for the home session as well. You have Silver Burdett's permission to duplicate the lyrics for use in the program.

Gestures   Ask the children to make appropriate gestures, such as holding hands with one another, as they sing. Join the group yourself. Tell them that you are friends, that you all belong to one another because you are all a part of God's family.

Prayer   Invite the children to stand for a concluding prayer. Help them become still and thoughtful. You might introduce the prayer with these words. "Let us close our eyes for a moment. We want to speak to the Lord.

"Let us pray: Lord, we thank you with all our hearts. You have given to each of us a family. We thank you for our parents. We thank you for our brothers and sisters. For all these gifts, we will sing for you."

Ask the children to hold hands and sing Song 1 on the record once more.

Reminders
Name Tags   Ask the children to return their name tags as they leave. Tell them the tags will be used again for the solemn inscription of the names of the candidates for First Communion, which will take place in a liturgical celebration.

Attendance Records   Record the information that the children have told you about themselves through varied activities. For example, you might note their address, the number of children in their family, and any special family situations that are pertinent to your understanding of the children.

The following activities are suggested for teachers who have time, perhaps even in a second group session, to give a fuller presentation of this theme or who would like to consider alternatives that might have particular appeal to this group. *Complementary Activities*

☼ Introduce the children to the first celebration. Obtain a copy of *Celebrations* and do some of the introductory activities on pages 1–2.

☼ Show a film or tell a story about belonging. Then use the film or story in order to begin a discussion of belonging.

Films
Nobody Important. TeleKETICS. 11 min., color.
Palle Alone in the World. Rembrandt Film Library. 20 min., b&w.

Books for Storytelling
Brown, Margaret Wise. *Runaway Bunny.* New York: Harper & Row, 1942; $3.95.
Charlip, Remy and Lillian Moore. *Hooray for Me!* New York: Parents' Magazine Press, 1975; $4.95.
Cohen, Miriam. *Will I Have a Friend?* New York: Macmillan, 1967; paper, $1.25.
Eastman, Philip. *Are You My Mother?* New York: Random House, 1967; $4.99 (English and Spanish).
Lionni, Leo. *Little Blue and Little Yellow.* Stamford, Conn.: Astor-Honor, 1959; $4.95.
———. *Swimmy.* New York: Pantheon, 1963; $5.99.
Mallett, Anne. *Here Comes Tagalong.* New York: Parents' Magazine Press, 1971; $4.95.
Reyher, Becky. *My Mother Is the Most Beautiful Woman in the World.* New York: Lothrop, Lee & Shepard, 1945; $5.61.
Scott, Ann Herbert. *On Mother's Lap.* New York: McGraw-Hill, 1972; $4.95.
Walter, Mildred. *Lillie of Watts: A Birthday Discovery.* Los Angeles: Ward Ritchie Press, 1969; $3.95.
Young, Miriam. *Peas in a Pod.* New York: Putnam, 1971; $3.86.

☼ See the suggestions for the home session, below.

Home Session

Aim

To help your child realize that it is through his or her parents that he or she belongs to God's family

Review

Ask your child to show you what he or she did on pages 2 and 3 of the Communion book, the "golden book," and to tell you about it. Encourage him or her to take care of this book as a special gift to the Lord. He or she will carry it up to the altar in the Offertory Procession on Communion day.

Continue with an informal conversation about what you and your child have experienced during the first celebration and the solemn inscription of the Communion candidates. You might guide the dialogue along the following lines.

"Where did we go together? What did we do together? We presented you as a candidate for Holy Communion. You gave your name to the priest. Do you remember the questions the priest asked us and you? The priest told you that you are now a candidate for Holy Communion."

Many families belong to God's family.

To help your child recognize that God's family is made up of many families, point out that many people were in God's house to participate in the first celebration. You might ask your child to name some of the parents and children who were there. Recall what you did together in God's house. For example, you might point out that you all sang together. You listened together to the reading of God's words. All the parents there were invited to present their children as candidates for First Holy Communion. All those children belong to God's family. They, too, are preparing for their First Holy Communion. You will often join them in class and at the celebrations.

30

Ask your child to open the Communion book, the "golden book," to page 4. Read the text together. Witness to the joy you and your family shared when your child was born. Witness to the desire you had to have your child belong to God's family because you belong to God's family. Tell your child how you chose his or her name. Ask your child to write his or her name in the space on page 4. Tell your child that he or she was given this name as a member of God's family at baptism. This name was written in the parish register. Describe the details of the baptism: the church, its location, the date, who was there to welcome your child into God's house and family.

You became a member of God's family at your baptism.

The Baptismal Rite Together look at the artwork on page 5. Explain what the priest is doing. Name the people who are usually present at a baptism. Comment on the significance of the growing custom of members of the parish being present at a baptism.

Liturgical Emphasis

Amen Acclamation Tell your child that the liturgical acclamation *Amen* means "Yes, Lord, I believe in you. I trust in you. I belong to you." Explain that you have answered Amen for him or her many times. Now he or she is old enough to say Amen with you in God's house. Sing an Amen together.

Baptismal Font When you have the opportunity, point out to your child the baptismal font and the Paschal Candle in your church. Let your child examine the baptismal font. Tell your child that his or her baptismal candle was lit at the Paschal Candle, which represents Jesus.

Reading Read the texts on page 4 of the "golden book." Help your child recall the story of his or her name (see above). Ask him or her to write that name at the bottom of page 4. Then turn to page 6 and read the text with your child. Explain that God knows all his children by their names. He knows us all by our names because he loves us. We are all his children. We all belong to his family. Read once more God's words: "I have called you by your name: you are mine" (Isaiah 43:1).

Activities

Drawing Ask your child to express on page 7 what he or she knows about baptism. Make a few suggestions to help him or her visualize the ceremony of baptism—for example, parents bringing their child to God's house, parents holding their child over the baptismal font, the priest giving the baptismal candle to the parents.

31

Give your child a felt-tipped pen or wax crayons for drawing. Such tools can help your child toward exuberant, creative, and graphic expressions of ideas. Avoid giving rulers, ball-point pens, erasers, or lead pencils. Those tools inhibit expression.

For further insights into the place and value of drawing in religious education, you might read pages 19–21 of the Introduction.

Interpretation Ask your child to tell you about the picture when it is completed. Some specific questions might help his or her verbal expression. You might say, "Tell me about this. What are these people doing? What are the mother and father asking the priest for their child?"

An explanation of the purpose and value of picture interpretation is presented on pages 13–14 of the Introduction.

Writing Invite your child to write the names of the people or objects that appear in the picture. Assist your child if he or she needs help in writing. Your child might dictate to you the meaning of the drawing.

Prayer Ask your child to say the following prayer with you. "Lord, I thank you for being your child. Lord, you love me. You call me by my name. Lord, I sing to you, for I belong to your family."

Singing You and your child might sing together Song 1 on the record *We Celebrate the Eucharist.* Either use the album, if you have purchased it, or learn the song from your child. Perhaps the catechist has given him or her a copy of the words of the song to take home.

Pasting Give your child a picture of himself or herself or of your family and ask your child to paste it in the Communion book in the space provided.

Reminder
Please sign your child's book on pages 3 and 7.

Complementary Activities

Family Album Spend some time looking over the family photos. Discuss the pictures of grandparents, aunts, uncles, cousins—the extended family. Be sure to include pictures of your child's baptism if you have them. Talk about who was there, what you did, how you felt, and so on.

Godparents Encourage your child to contact his or her godparents, by note, visit, or telephone. It is not too early to ask their prayers for their godchild's initiation into the Eucharist. For your own part, you might suggest they make a First Communion present to your child in the form of the record *We Celebrate the Eucharist.*

Family Tree Diagram your extended family on a large sheet of paper, as far back as you can. You might wish to research the origin and meaning of your family name as well. As in all these activities, stress belonging to a family, and belonging to God's family.

Storytelling Listed on page 29 of this guide are a few books on the theme of belonging. You may wish to borrow some of those books from your library and read them with your child, or you may prefer to purchase some of them for your child's use.

The Eucharist:
It's About Celebrating

Celebrations are a fact of human existence; they serve a real human purpose, fulfill a truly human need. Margaret Mead, a contemporary anthropologist who has done extensive comparative studies of cultures, has written:

Celebrations answer the needs of each age: of the youngest child— first enthralled by the lights of candles on a cake or electrically lighted trees; or the older child beginning to remember and to forget his early childhood; of the adolescent hovering between a past that he must leave and a future that is not yet; of young parents, partly caught by memories of their parents; of grandmothers living again in the so different eyes of their grandchildren; of great-grandparents, living longer than people have ever lived and trying hard to remain in touch with the modern world. A celebration must be a ceremony in which each finds something of his own and all share something together. It must be a community ceremonial if it is to have a place for each of them.

And this is really something of what the Eucharist is about. From the earliest times Christians have felt that their life together is something worth celebrating, worth becoming deeply concerned about.

We Christians celebrate our fellowship and the reason for that fellowship: the active presence of Jesus Christ. The truth that nothing "will be able to separate us from the love of God that comes to us in Christ Jesus, our Lord" (Romans 8:39) has given us life and makes our lives worth celebrating.

Despite changes in the form of the Mass through the years, the meaning of the eucharistic gathering has always remained the same. When we come together in the Eucharist, we gather in celebration. We celebrate the fact that, in Jesus Christ, God our Father has freed us from slavery to ourselves in order that we may live before him here and now a life of concern for our brothers and sisters. We celebrate our belief that we are a people to whom Jesus Christ is present today—present for us in the gathered community, in his Word, in the bread. And we celebrate our hope that God our Father's absolute love for us, a love which has given us life, will not be confined but will give us "life to the full."

All the elements in the eucharistic celebration seek to reinforce the meaning of our gathering. But certain elements, particular prayers and actions, signify in a special way that this gathering is more than a mere crowd of people.

The church building, which allows everyone to come together as a single group in one place, points to the purposefulness of our gathering. The centers of interest within the building make evident the related ways in which Christ, the cause of the fellowship we celebrate, is really present to us: in the gathered community (the church itself), in the person of the priest (the place of the presiding celebrant), in the Word (the lectern or pulpit), in the bread and the cup (the Lord's table).

The singing that usually accompanies the entrance procession is meant to nourish our unity, to help each of us become more aware of our community with those who gather with us. The opening dialogue establishes communication and fosters unity between the celebrant and the congregation. The greeting by the priest is a further sign of the active presence of Christ, who invites us to this time of sharing. The opening prayer helps to unite our assembly, to unite the individuals in one common prayer that expresses the character of the celebration. All these elements work together to give us at the start that sense of oneness so necessary for the celebration of our one life.

Although we may and do celebrate the Eucharist on any day, we have come to identify this celebration in a special way with Sunday.

In the Old Testament, God reserved a day of rest and renewal for his people. This day also served as a special day of celebration in God's honor (Exodus 20:9-11). In the New Testament, Christians chose Sunday to celebrate the cause of their fellowship: the life-giving presence of the Lord Jesus (Acts 20:7).

Today as well, we Christians respond on the Lord's Day to Christ's invitation to celebrate our birth to a new life begun in baptism and nourished now in the Eucharist. There even exists a Church precept that serves to underline the importance of the human need that is served through this celebration.

We generally experience the whole of Sunday as a special day. In our culture, Sunday is a time to rest, to relax, to find oneself anew. Such an experience of Sunday can only serve to enhance and support our Christian experience of Sunday, for it, too, is a special experience of rediscovery and re-creation—of God's family and all the families within it. Whatever the family does on Sunday or at any time to renew its life contributes to the meaning of our Christian celebration of shared life. And this celebration, which serves as the core of our Sundays, in turn adds to the renewal of each family in a most profound way.

The Eucharist is indeed a celebration in the deepest sense. It was originally intended to be so, and has remained so. Accordingly, we must ask ourselves from time to time if we do experience the Eucharist as a real celebration. To do so does not demand that we know each person with whom we celebrate. It does not require the noisy and sometimes frenzied participation appropriate for a football game. It does not require the casualness of a backyard cookout. But it does call for a climate of openness with one another, of caring, and of rejoicing. It presupposes a deep realization that we are people who belong together, saved and called by Christ.

Group Session

Aim

To help the children realize that every family keeps special days to celebrate the life and the love they share with one another

Review

To begin this session and to show the joy of belonging to the Communion group, you might sing with the children Song 1 on the record *We Celebrate the Eucharist,* all holding hands. Ask the children to tell you about, and show you, the work they did at home on page 7 of the Communion book.

Ask the children if they celebrate special *events* in their families or neighborhoods. Ask them to name some events they celebrate (birthdays, anniversaries, family reunions) and to tell why those events are celebrated. Encourage them to describe family celebrations they have taken part in. Ask them how they feel at such celebrations.

Families celebrate special occasions.

Ask the children if there are special *days* during the year that their family likes to celebrate (Christmas, Thanksgiving Day, Fourth of July). Discuss what they usually do on those occasions. They might mention that they have special food and wear special clothing, that special people are invited, that they play special games and sing special songs, that there are decorations and flowers.

Conclude this discussion by leading your group in a song usually sung to express joy when we celebrate a happy event—for example, "Happy Birthday."

Ask the children why Sunday is a special day of the week. Discuss what is special about Sunday. Help the children recognize that Sunday is often a day of family joy and rest. You might cover the following points.

Sunday is a day for family celebration.

Nobody has to go to school on Sunday. Most mothers and fathers stay at home. We do special things. We may go to a park, a fair, or a zoo. We may have a picnic, go hiking, visit friends or relatives. We may have a special meal, such as brunch or a cookout.

Activities

Picture Discussion Ask the children to open their book to pages 8 and 9 and to look at the pictures. Discuss what is happening in each picture. Emphasize the joy of celebrating together. You might ask questions such as, "How can you tell that the two children in the first [or third] picture are having fun? What are some of the fun things you do on Sundays? What might the girl in the second picture be saying to her mother? What do you like best about birthday parties? What does your family like most to do together on Sundays? Look at the children in the last picture. What do you like to do when you are really happy? How do you celebrate?"

Reading Ask the children to turn to page 10 and to read the text. If the children need help in reading, you might read the page aloud as the children follow.

Writing Ask the children to fill in the spaces on page 10 with appropriate responses.

Drawing Distribute wax crayons or felt-tipped pens. Ask the children to draw on page 11 a picture of the celebration they remember best and especially enjoyed. Encourage the children to describe their experiences.

Interpretation As the children complete their drawings, speak privately with each one. Ask them to identify by name each person in the drawing. Ask some specific questions to help them describe what they are expressing. You might ask, "What celebration have you drawn? Who is this? Who is that? What are these people using in the celebration? How does everybody feel? How do you feel in your picture? Why?"

Singing Teach Song 2 on the record *We Celebrate the Eucharist*. (See page 16 of the Introduction, above, for suggestions on how to teach the children songs.) If you wish, give the children each a copy of the lyrics to take home. You have Silver Burdett's permission to duplicate the lyrics for use in the program. In this way the song can be used in the home session as well.

Celebration Have a small celebration within your group to express the happiness and joy that you share as friends. Create a festive atmosphere with whatever you have available. You might provide balloons, paper hats, and some musical instruments. By all means, share some cookies or cake.

Prayer Close the friendship celebration by singing the antiphon or by having the children repeat after you this prayer: "Lord, we thank you for giving us our family to celebrate with. Lord, we thank you for giving us our friends to celebrate with. Lord, we thank you for giving us so many special days for celebrations."

Reminder

Attendance Records After the session, fill in the attendance record for each child.

Complementary Activities

⚙ If you have extra time, perhaps even the opportunity for another group session, you might introduce the children to the second celebration. Obtain a copy of the *Celebrations* book and use the top portion of page 11.

⚙ Show a film, or retell (or read) a story. Here are some suggestions.

Films
Either of the following films might be used to introduce the theme of the celebration of Sunday. The teachers might assemble all the children in the program to view one of these films before starting their group discussion. If a film is shown, the discussion that follows should be directly related to what has been seen.

Jenny's Birthday. Weston Woods Studios. 8 min., b&w and color.
Stefan on Sunday. Encyclopaedia Britannica Educational Corp. 14 min., color.
This Sunday Party. Thomas S. Klise Co. 19 min., color [filmstrip].

Books for Storytelling
You might choose one of the following books to read to your group and then use it to enhance the presentation of Theme 2.

Hoban, Russell. *A Birthday for Frances*. New York: Harper & Row, 1968; $3.95.

L'Engle, Madeleine. *Dance in the Desert*. New York: Farrar, Straus & Giroux, 1969; $4.95.

☼ See the suggestions for the home session, below.

Home Session

To help your child realize that every week your whole family is invited to celebrate the day of the Lord

Aim

Review what has been done on the theme of celebrating. You might read and discuss the text on page 10. You might ask your child to describe the drawings on page 11, or to tell you all he or she remembers about the liturgical celebration you attended together.

Review

Discuss the special things that you do as a family on weekends. Explain how important it is for a family to take time every week to celebrate the love and unity that exist among its members. Stress everyone's joy at the presence of those in the family who cannot always be present during the week. Stress also the joy of breaking the work routine of the week, of having time for play, family activities, cookouts, special visitors, and special visits.

God asks us to celebrate the day of the Lord.

Tell your child in your own words that God knows we need a day each week to rest from our work. God knows that we need to take a full day for family joy, just for being together and for sharing our love with one another. Ask your child to listen to the Word of God. Read the following adaptation of Exodus 20:8-11.

"Remember that the seventh day is a special day. It is the day of the Lord. On that day, rest from work and enjoy the world which I have made for you. On that day, sing and rejoice, celebrate life, for this is my special day. It is called the day of the Lord."

41

God invites us to his celebration.

Turn to page 12 in the "golden book" and read the first column.

Explain that God wants us to celebrate with him and with his family in his house. Every week we are invited to come to God's house for a feast. God hopes that we will answer his invitation with a joyful Yes.

Discuss how your family answers God's invitation by reviewing the concrete preparations you make before going to Mass.

Liturgical Emphasis

Entrance Procession and Song Turn to page 13 in the "golden book." Encourage your child to express what the picture suggests to him or her. Explain that we sing a song at the beginning of Mass to show our joy to the Lord. You might sing together Song 2 on the record *We Celebrate the Eucharist.*

Describe how people at Mass welcome the celebrant with songs of praise and joy. Ask your child why he or she thinks this is done. Help your child understand that the celebrant comes among us in the name of the Lord.

The Greeting Tell your child that after the singing the celebrant greets us with the words "The Lord be with you." We reply, "And also with you." Teach your child to answer the celebrant's greeting.

The Gloria Explain that after the song and the greeting all the people want to tell about God's great glory and goodness. They say or sing a special prayer called the Gloria. Read with your child the second column of page 12.

Activities

Reading Read with your child Jesus' words on page 14 and the paragraphs that follow.

Writing Ask your child to fill in the spaces on page 14 with the names of some of the people you meet at church.

Drawing Direct your child to make a drawing on page 15 of what he or she experiences (sees and enjoys doing) when he or she goes with you to God's house to celebrate with God's family.

Interpretation When your child has completed this work (do not accept work that has been done carelessly), ask him or her to show it to you and tell you about it. As always, specific questions will lead to fruitful results. You might ask, for example, "Who are these people? Where are they going? What special things do we see in God's house? What special things do people do in God's house?"

Singing Sing Song 2 on the record *We Celebrate the Eucharist.* Use the album if you have it, or learn it from your child, who may have been given a copy of the lyrics to take home.

Reminder
Please sign your child's book on pages 11 and 15.

Prayer We suggest that you pray all or part of the Gloria with your child during the week at bedtime. It is important that your child be progressively trained to say or sing the prayers that are recited by the adult community at Mass. It would be a liturgical and psychological error to try to adapt these prayers to the children's vocabulary. If we were to simplify the prayers, we would make it difficult for children to share fully in the prayers of God's people.

Complementary Activities

Storytelling You might read to your child one or both of the stories on the theme of celebrating that are recommended on page 40 of this guide, or another story about celebrating.

Special Events Make a list of the events your family celebrates. Talk about why they are so special. Indicate their dates.

Calendar Make a calendar of special family dates (or mark a calendar). Include birthdays, anniversaries, holidays, and special holy days.

Album Spend some time looking at family pictures taken on these special days.

Birthday Present Plan a birthday present for someone whose birthday might be coming up soon.

Grace Pray a family grace before the Sunday meal. Ask your child to compose this prayer of thanksgiving.

The Eucharist:

It's About Making Peace

From the dawn of Judeo-Christian history, the oneness of God's people was accepted as a gift from God. It was God who formed Israel into one people in the desert. The law that he gave them in the Old Testament was not only a sign of his concern for them, but also a source of their unity in him. To violate God's law was to disrupt the community, and this meant sinning against God himself.

When the covenant between God and the human race was fulfilled in Christ, a new people was formed. Their law goes far beyond the legal. It is crystallized in the Sermon on the Mount, in the Beatitudes, which call upon people to share the spirit of Christ—a spirit of love, of justice, of truth, of patience, of forgiveness. To refuse a respond to this call not only weakens the bonds of fellowship but also strains our relationship with God. We Christians know that whatever we do to build up or tear down the human community also profoundly affects our relationship to the Father and Creator of all people. When we recognize this fundamental truth, we are taking seriously Christ's words: "As often as you did it for one of my least brothers, you did it for me" (Matthew 25:40). Only if we take these words very seriously can we begin to build a world neighborhood.

INTRODUCTION TO THE THEME

45

It should not be at all surprising that our celebration of life together, our concern for building a world neighborhood and our concern for everything we do that impedes it, finds expression in the Eucharist. The entire eucharistic liturgy, as the whole of our Christian lives, points toward unity. But certain elements of the eucharistic liturgy make this concern more evident. These elements are the *Penitential Rite,* in which we seek the forgiveness of God and of one another for our failure to foster the unity he gives us; the *Prayer of the Faithful,* in which we pray for the needs of the human family; and the *Sign of Peace,* in which we show both the oneness we have and the oneness we seek in the Eucharist.

The Penitential Rite appears in our celebration as a moment of honesty, of sober realism—always needed, though perhaps not always welcome. In this rite, we confess openly to one another and to God our failure to respond to his gift of unity. In it we seek the forgiveness of our Father and of our brothers and sisters. The priest then pronounces absolution, God's word of forgiving love.

The inclusion of this rite in the celebration serves as a reminder that the Eucharist is a great moment in our Christian awareness of evil and sin in our lives and in the world. And it recalls to us the sometimes forgotten truth that, in this celebration, Christ, through the ministry of the priest, truly forgives our daily sins, our failures in building up the human community.

The Prayer of the Faithful deserves separate consideration because of its added character of response to the Word of God. It is considered in Theme 5.

The Sign of Peace takes place within the Communion rite. In recent years, this rite has been restored to its former place as an action of deep significance in the liturgy. Both a prayer and a gesture make up the Sign of Peace. First of all, the priest prays in the name of the gathered community for the peace and unity that only the risen Lord Jesus can bring. In this way, we recognize both the source of our unity and the fact that we have not yet fully experienced the peace that accompanies it. Then we exchange with one another a greeting of peace. This gesture is a sign of our willingness to be united with one another despite any differences we may have. It is a pledge of our mutual love before we share in the one bread, the sign of the love that nourishes us.

Though each of these rites takes place within a different movement of the eucharistic celebration, they are very closely related. In each rite we recognize who we are now and who we are called to be. In each we admit that we have fallen short of our task, that we are at a distance from our goal, and we offer a pledge for the future. Through each God speaks to us, offering to restore or strengthen his gift of unity.

Each rite offers us a way of responding to Christ's words. "If you bring your gift to the altar and there recall that your brother has anything against you, leave your gift at the altar, go first to be reconciled with your brother, and then come and offer your gift" (Matthew 5:23-24). Each rite offers Christ a means of fulfilling his promise. " 'Peace' is my farewell to you, my peace is my gift to you" (John 14:27).

In a world at once more united yet more fragmented than ever, the concern that these rites express and the promise that they fulfill in the Eucharist should speak to us in a special way. They show us something of what our Christian Eucharist is really all about: reconciling. And reconciling is about making peace.

Group Session

To help the children realize that to be happy they need people's loving mercy and forgiveness, and that they themselves need to forgive and make peace with others

Aim

Greet each child with special love and concern. Review the preceding lesson on celebrating with God's family. Ask the children to show you the work they did on pages 14 and 15 of their book and to tell you about it.

Review

Open this topic by discussing a few examples of situations in which people do not get along with one another. Sometimes people in a family, at school, or in a neighborhood have "arguments" with one another. They quarrel, fight, pout, hurt one another with unkind words, and refuse to speak to one another. Explain that everyone feels very unhappy when this happens in a family or in a neighborhood.

Quarreling causes unhappiness.

Ask the children to open their "golden book" to pages 16 and 17 and to look at the first picture. Ask what might have made the little boy so un-

47

happy. How do they feel, seeing him look so unhappy? Then ask them if they sometimes quarrel, fight, pout. Use specific questions. "How do you feel about quarreling? How do you feel about fighting? Do you ever pout when things don't go your way? What can you do about quarreling? about fighting? about pouting?"

Our parents are willing to forgive us.

Speak with the children about the wrongs they may do at home and about their parents' willingness to forgive them. Use concrete examples and specific details. The following may serve as a model.

"Sometimes we make our parents unhappy because we have done something wrong. We may refuse to help. We may say, 'I won't do my homework.' We may be mean to a brother or sister. When this happens, our parents are not happy. We are not happy either down deep in our heart. One of our parents' greatest joys is to have us tell them we are sorry and will try never to disobey or be mean again. They are ready to forgive us. They forget all about the wrong thing we have done. Once again we are a happy family."

Others are also willing to forgive us.

Ask the children to look at the picture of the boy and his father on page 16. Tell them that this father is ready to forget whatever has happened. Then ask the children if this has ever happened to them.

Ask the children if they can describe situations in which people besides their parents were willing to forgive them. You might ask, "Can you tell us about a time when you told your brother or sister you were sorry for something you had done and you made up? Can you tell us about a time when you made up with a friend? Do you ever get into trouble in school? Do you ever tell your teacher that you are sorry? Does your teacher forgive you?"

Ask the children to look at the picture of the two boys walking down the street. Explain that these boys share love and peace with each other. Ask the children how they can tell that the boys are happy together.

Then ask them to look at the picture of the handshake. Ask them to describe how they think the two people feel.

I should always forgive others.

Ask the children about their readiness to forgive someone who has done something wrong to them. Ask if they can remember a time when they made up with someone after a quarrel. Ask how they made up, how they felt after they had made up. Help the children come to some appreciation of the peace and joy that come with reconciliations.

48

Reading   Ask the children to turn to page 18 of their book and to read the text. If your situation requires it, you might read the text to or with the children. Welcome their comments and questions, and let the group reflect on any points that are made by individuals.

Writing   Ask the children to fill in the spaces with their own responses to the two questions on page 18.

Drawing   Ask the children to draw a picture on page 19 of a reconciliation they have experienced. Suggest that they show what making up meant to them, and how happy they were after peace was restored.

If any children prefer to write a story rather than tell it through a picture, let them do so.

Interpretation   As soon as a child completes the drawing or story, invite him or her to show it to you and tell you about it. Help the children express themselves by asking them simple, direct questions. For example, "Who is this person? Why is he (she) in your picture? How did you feel about what happened between you? How did you feel after you had made up?"

Discussion   Consider ways people make up and restore peace with one another. Explain that people show their reconciliation in different ways. Ask the children what their parents may do when they want to show that they have forgiven them. "Do your parents hug you and kiss you? How do you show your brother or sister that you have made up? What do you do when you make peace with a friend?"

Singing   Teach Song 3 on the record *We Celebrate the Eucharist*. You may wish to refer to our suggestions for teaching songs on page 16, above. Duplicate the lyrics if you wish, so that the children may take them home to sing in the home session.

Prayer   Lead the children in the following meditative prayer. "Lord, it is not always easy to ask forgiveness and to make peace with one another. Give us your Spirit of unity and peace. Your Spirit can change our hearts."

Then you may wish to repeat part of the song you have learned.

Reminder
Attendance Records   After the session, fill in the record that you are keeping on each child.

Activities

Complementary Activities

☸ If you wish to do so and have the time, introduce your children to the third celebration. Obtain a copy of *Celebrations* and follow the directions on pages 19–20.

☸ If you wish, show a film, or tell or read a story. Here are some suggestions.

Films

God Waits for Me. Roa Films. 25 min., color.

Half Inch of Selfishness. Roa Films. 15 min., b&w.

The King and the Lion. Contemporary Films/McGraw-Hill. 12 min., color.

Let's Make Up. Thomas S. Klise Co. 19 min., color [filmstrip].

Little Blue and Little Yellow. Contemporary Films/McGraw-Hill. 10 min., color.

Books for Storytelling

Beim, Lorraine and Jerrald. *Two is a Team*. New York: Harcourt Brace Jovanovich, 1945; $6.50. Paper, 1974; $1.25.

Bonsall, Crosby. *It's Mine*. New York: Harper and Row, 1964; $3.79.

Bulla, Clyde Robert. *The Poppy Seeds*. New York: Crowell, 1955; $4.50.

Crippen, David. *Two Sides of the River*. Nashville: Abingdon, 1977; $4.25.

Haywood, Carolyn. *Betsy and the Boys*. New York: Harcourt Brace Jovanovich, 1945; $6.95.

Pottebaum, Gerard A. *99 Plus One*. Minneapolis, Minn.: Augsburg, 1971; $3.50.

Viorst, Judith. *Rosie and Michael*. New York: Atheneum, 1974; $6.95.

Zolotow, Charlotte. *The Hating Book*. New York: Harper and Row, 1969; $3.95.

☸ Consult the suggestions for the home session, below.

Home Session

Aim

To help your child realize that in God's family we are forgiven and reconciled with God and with our brothers and sisters

Review

Ask your child to tell you about the work he or she did in class. Discuss his or her drawing or story on page 19 of the "golden book."

If you know that the need for reconciliation exists between your child and a playmate, a member of your family, or someone in your neighborhood, this is a good opportunity for you to help him or her talk about it and for you to point out that reconciliation brings joy and peace. Help your child see the positive and expansive values in forgiving and making up.

With your child, look at the pictures on pages 16 and 17 of the "golden book." Pause for a moment at each picture. Ask your child to describe how he or she thinks the boy in the first picture feels.

Parents forgive their children.

"What might have made this boy sad? How do you feel toward him? What might help him now? What do you think is happening in the second picture? How does the third picture make you feel? Have you ever felt the way the boys in this picture feel? What is the fourth picture saying?"

Describe your joy when your child comes to you to ask forgiveness after something has gone wrong. Explain that parents are willing to forgive their children over and over again because they love them, and the love they have in their heart comes from God.

Explain that God is willing to forgive us over and over again when we ask his forgiveness. Use Matthew 18:21-22 to help you make your presentation specific and detailed. You might base your account on the following adaptation.

God also forgives his children.

"One day Peter, who was a very good friend of Jesus', came to Jesus and asked, 'Lord, how many times can my brother hurt me and how many times do I have to forgive him? Should I forgive him seven times?' (To Peter this seemed like a lot!)

"Jesus looked at his friend Peter and said, 'No, not seven times, but seventy times seven. You should forgive your brother or sister over and over again.'"

Then help your child assimilate this story by asking questions such as these: "How do you think Peter felt about Jesus' words? What do you think about Jesus' words? Do you think what Jesus asked Peter is too hard to do? Why? Why not?"

Ask your child to listen to what happened another time; then retell Matthew 6:14-15.

"Early one morning Jesus went out all by himself to pray. When he came back, his friends said to him, 'Lord, teach us how to pray.' Jesus taught them how to pray to their heavenly Father. He taught them many beautiful words. Some of Jesus' words tell us about forgiveness. Listen to the words of Jesus: 'Father, forgive us our trespasses as we forgive those who trespass against us.' "

Reflect with your child for a few minutes on whether we always obey Jesus' words; whether we are always ready to forgive and make peace with those who do us wrong. Ask your child to open his or her book to page 20. Read the first paragraph together. Comment briefly on what you have read, and encourage your child to express his or her thoughts.

Liturgical Emphasis **The Penitential Rite** Help your child recall the particular actions—that is, the special prayers, songs, and gestures—that are part of the liturgical celebration in which people ask forgiveness of God and one another. You might mention the following. The celebrant invites us to remember our sins. We ask God's and one another's forgiveness. The celebrant expresses God's forgiveness of our daily sins. He traces over us the sign of the cross and says, "May almighty God have mercy on us, forgive us our sins and bring us to everlasting life."

Explain that we ask the Lord's forgiveness by saying or singing, "Lord, have mercy." Read or sing with your child "Lord, have mercy," page 20 of the "golden book."

The Sign of Peace Discuss the picture on page 21. Show your child how we give the sign of peace to our brothers and sisters in God's house. Teach him or her the words that go with the gesture. They are on page 20.

Activities **Reading** Read the text on page 22 of your child's book, and comment briefly on it.

Drawing Give your child crayons and ask him or her to draw a picture on page 23 of the sign of peace that we give to one another in God's house during the celebration.

Interpretation When your child has finished the drawing, ask him or her to show it to you and tell you about it. As always, specific questions will lead to the best verbal expression. You might ask, for example, "Who are these people? Where are they? What are they doing? What do they say to one another when they give the Sign of Peace?"

Prayer Ask your child to repeat each sentence after you: "Lord, it is not always easy to ask forgiveness. Give me your strength to forgive those who do wrong to me. Give me your Spirit of peace to make peace with others. Change my heart with your Spirit of love."

Singing You might wish to end this home session by singing together Song 3 on the record *We Celebrate the Eucharist*. Play the record if you have it, or let your child teach you the song.

Reminder
Please sign your child's book on pages 19 and 23.

Storytelling You might read to your child one or more of the stories suggested on page 50, above, and then relate the material to what you have considered together about making peace.

Complementary Activities

Word-Portrait Game It is essential that parents join in this activity and set a light and friendly tone. Explain that the purpose of the game is not to criticize, but "to see ourselves as others see us" (Robert Burns).

Each player—as many family members as possible—gets as many sheets of paper as there are players, less one.

Each sheet has three headings: (1) This is a portrait of_____. (2) What I like most about_____is: (3) I would like to see_____change in this way:

Each player fills out a sheet on each of the others. When all have finished, each player collects all the sheets pertaining to himself or herself and reads them privately.

If a player so desires, the sheets pertaining to him or her may be read aloud. If this is done, care must be taken that the friendly spirit of this game does not deteriorate into one of fault-finding. When carried out in a spirit of love and with a sense of humor, this activity can be the occasion of a deepening of the confidence one has in the other members of the family.

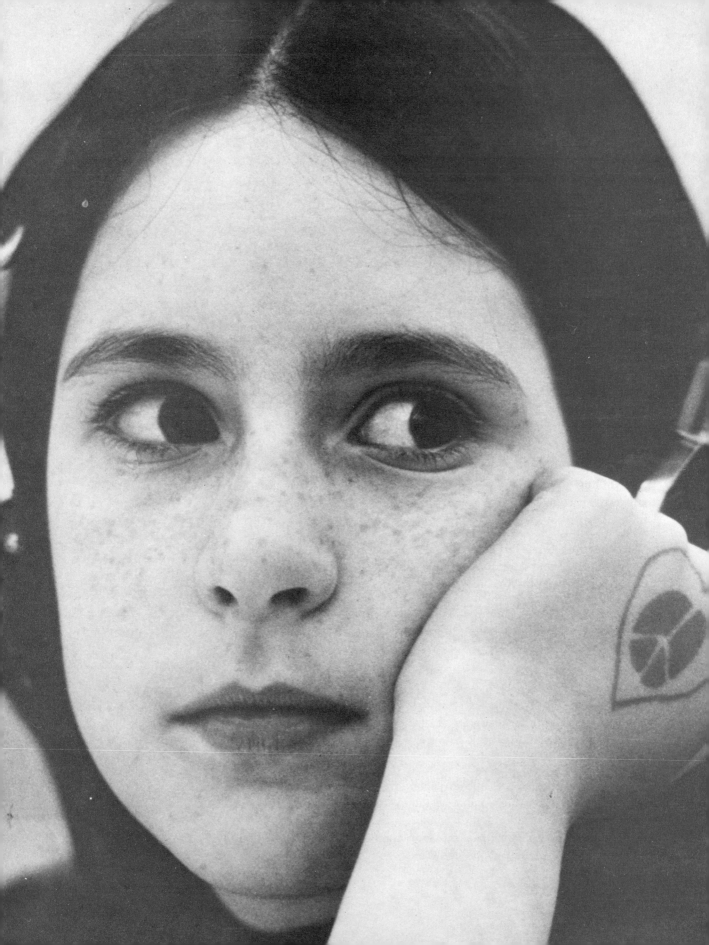

The Eucharist:
It's About Listening

Listening is of the utmost importance in our Christian lives. We are summoned to listen to the continuing expression of God's love through the risen Christ.

Jesus Christ is present in his Church, summoning men and women to become witnesses to his resurrection and life. He is present when the community gathers in response to his call. He is present in the sacraments to express his love. He is present in his Word when Scripture is read in his Church.

To listen for the risen Christ, to be attentive as he speaks to us today, requires a good deal of perception, a large measure of patience, and most of all, Christian faith. Listening for the living Christ is an activity, not a mechanical process or a passive performance.

The gospel accounts mention that Jesus and his disciples themselves participated in this synagogue liturgy of listening to God's Word in the Scriptures (Mark 1:39; Matthew 4:23; Luke 4:16-22; John 6:59). On one such occasion Christ introduced a new dimension to God's design for his people.

He came to Nazareth where he had been reared, and entering the synagogue on the sabbath as he was in the habit of doing, he stood up to do the reading. When the book of the prophet Isaiah was handed him, he unrolled the scroll and found the passage where it was written:

> *The Spirit of the Lord is upon me;*
> *therefore he has anointed me.*
> *He has sent me to bring glad tidings*
> *to the poor,*
> *to proclaim liberty to captives,*
> *Recovery of sight to the blind*
> *and release to prisoners,*
> *To announce a year of favor from the Lord.*

Rolling up the scroll he gave it back to the assistant and sat down. All in the synagogue had their eyes fixed on him. Then he began by saying to them, "Today this Scripture passage is fulfilled in your hearing." All who were present spoke favorably of him; they marveled at the appealing discourse which came from his lips (Luke 4:16-22).

The traditional liturgy of the synagogue served as the framework within which Jesus, in the context of the commentary on the reading, inserted a new dimension—one that is specifically Christian: he announced the fulfillment of the words of the Law and the summons of the prophets. He took this occasion of patient listening and spoke a new word: he announced the gospel, the "good news." He proclaimed the word of liberation and invited his hearers to lend a responsive ear.

One day this new dimension that Jesus had brought to the lives of those around him would find its way into their own liturgy. It would be crystallized in the gospel accounts and in the letters of some early Christians; it would be read in Christian gatherings along with the Word of the same God of former times. These gatherings would be marked by a spirit of attentive listening, founded on the belief that the same Christ who spoke this new Word was truly alive and continued to manifest the Father's love.

In the second century, this gathering was incorporated into the Sunday celebration of the Eucharist; and by the fourth century, it had become a feature of every such celebration. Readings from Scripture, the Word of God, formed the core of the fore-Mass in the liturgy. Hence it is often called the Liturgy of the Word.

The form of the Liturgy of the Word today shows the influence of this historical development. And the rhythm of "hearing and responding" underlines the fact that for Christians, listening is something we do, not something that happens to us.

The Entrance Liturgy, which through song, dialogue, and prayer has served to draw us together, also prepares us to listen to God, who speaks to us. This first movement of our celebration opens us to the presence of Christ in the Word.

First, through a reading from the Old Testament, we hear once again the Word that God spoke in Israel. We respond to this Word, which represents the beginning of God's explicit call to his people, by singing the responsorial psalm. In this way, we seek to make God's Word our own.

Then we hear the apostles tell us what it means truly to listen to the Word of God and to welcome his Word as a living force in our lives. After the reading of the epistle, we rise to welcome the Word of God. Through our Alleluia, we acclaim Christ, who announces the "good news," in a reading from the gospel accounts. In the homily that follows, the celebrant tries to help us understand the Word of God as an expression of love for us and to respond to God's Word in love.

The Creed offers us a means of assenting to the Word of God that we have heard in the lessons and the homily. Its place in the celebration also indicates why we include the Liturgy of the Word within the celebration of the Eucharist: that Christians should be nourished at the table of the Word before they are nourished at the sacramental table. The Eucharist is celebrated fully only in faith, and it is the Word of God that gives rise to that faith. Hearing the sacred Word, commemorating what God has done among us, is really our best preparation for his continuing action of love for us, which is the gift of his Son in the Eucharist.

Within the eucharistic celebration, the proclamation of the Word of the living God becomes a contemporary challenge, an invitation today to open our ears and our hearts to the Lord who speaks, a summons to continue the meaning of Jesus Christ in our world. For the Christian who has heard the "good news," listening is indeed a full-time job.

Group Session

Aim   To help the children develop their capacity for listening attentively

Review   Greet each child personally. Review the preceding lesson on forgiving and making peace. Ask the children to show you their work on page 23 of their book, and discuss it with them. Encourage the children to express freely any further insights into Theme 3 that they may wish to share with the group.

We listen to sounds.   Invite the children to close their eyes and open their ears so that they may listen attentively to the sounds that surround them. After a few seconds, ask each child to describe the specific sounds he or she has heard.

Tell the children that you would now like to show them how they can become completely still so that they may listen even more attentively. Direct them to put their hands flat on their knees, keep their body straight, keep their feet quiet, and close their eyes. Have them repeat this exercise after you.

Permit the children to relax for a moment; then repeat this exercise in listening. Explain that they are now ready to listen to more sounds. Ask the children to name the sounds they now hear. Tell them about the sounds that you hear. Then tell the children that you are going to make three sounds. They are to listen and try to identify each sound. Ask them to close their eyes. Stand behind the children and make some sounds familiar to them. For example, crumple a piece of paper in your hand, rattle some coins in your pocket, wind your watch, jangle some keys. Ask the children to identify and describe each sound that you have made.

We listen to words.   Read the children a short poem in which sounds suggest meanings, or play a recording of a song that has a catchy air. Then ask the children if they can tell you a few words of the poem or pantomime the action implied in the words of the song. If they are unable to answer, repeat the exercise. Your group may need more time and practice to become

58   attentive listeners.

You might select a song such as "This Old Man." Some appropriate poems are "Ice" by Dorothy Aldis, "The Baby Goes to Boston" by Laura E. Richards, and "The Big Clock" (author unknown). All of these poems are found in *The Arbuthnot Anthology of Children's Literature,* new ed., compiled by May Hill Arbuthnot (Glenview, Ill.: Scott, Foresman, 1961).

Have the children name some sounds they hear at home. Then ask them to describe sounds they associate with the presence of people they love; for example, the sound of their parents' car entering the driveway, the sounds from the kitchen when their mother or father is preparing breakfast, the sound of the doorbell announcing a relative's arrival, the call of a friend coming to play. *We listen to people.*

Now direct your discussion to listening to people themselves. Speak about what often happens in a family in which people love one another. You might use the example of a father returning home from work or from a business trip. Describe how he likes to take time to listen to his wife and children. They tell him about the many things that happened during the day at home and at school. Point out that the mother and children like to listen too. Mother likes to hear her husband, and the children their father, tell about the people he met and the things he saw and did. Or if mother or one of the older children is away for the day (or longer), the rest of the family want to hear what he or she did, saw, and experienced. The traveler, too, wants to listen—to the things the others did while he or she was away. Most often this news is shared at the dinner table when the family is gathered for a meal.

Picture Discussion Ask the children to open their book and look at the pictures on pages 24 and 25. Encourage them to discuss and respond to the pictures. You might ask the children to select one picture and to tell a story about it. Or you might consider each picture with them. You might use the following guidelines in your presentation. *Activities*

"Look at the girl in the first picture. She is wearing earphones. Have you ever used earphones? What did you listen to with earphones? What is happening in the second picture? What might the boy be telling his mother? How can you tell his mother is really listening?

Continue by saying, "Now look at the picture of the girl with her teacher. Do you think the girl is listening very hard? Tell us about times when you listen to your teacher. Who do you think is reading to the girl in the last picture? What book is he reading to her? What do you like best about listening to stories? Whom do you like to have read stories to you?"

Reading   Read the text on page 26 to the children, or ask several children to read it. Pause after each sentence to allow some reflection and reaction on the part of the children.

Writing   Distribute crayons or felt-tipped pens. Ask the children to think once again before filling in the spaces on page 26 with the names of the things and people they like to listen to most.

Drawing   Ask the children to draw a picture of a person they like to listen to. Encourage them to express their thoughts freely.

If any children prefer to write a story about a person they like to listen to, let them do so. You might play soft background music during this activity.

Interpretation   Invite each child to show you his or her work and tell you about it as soon as it is completed. Help them express themselves. Use specific questions, such as, "Who is this person? Why do you like to listen to him (her)? Does he (she) teach you things you like to know? things you like to do?"

Demonstration   Ask the children if they often listen to stories either at home or in school. Explain that when people write books they tell us things they want us to know about. From books we can learn about people, places, and things.

Then tell the children that you want to show them a very special book. Reverently place a Bible where all the children can see it. Tell them that this special book is called a Bible. God's words are written in the Bible. The Bible tells us about God's love for us and all he does for people. It is the most important book that has ever been written.

Take the Bible in your hands and show the children that there are two main parts to the Bible: the Old Testament and the New Testament. Explain that in the Old Testament we read about God's love for us and what he does for us. In the New Testament we read about the life of Jesus, the Son of God, and all that he does for people.

60   **Singing**   Tell the children that you would like to teach them a song of

joy about listening to God's Word at Mass. Teach Song 4 on the record *We Celebrate the Eucharist.*

Song 4 is a little different from the others. Verse A has pauses for listening, during which you might jingle keys, crumple paper, and the like, as above. Then in Verse B the singers sing the name of the sound they heard—"Ke-e-ys rattling, that's what I heard!" or "Paper crumpling, that's what I heard!" or whatever the sound was. Of course you must guide the singers for the exact wording. Verses A and B can alternate indefinitely, with new sounds introduced each time.

Prayer Ask the children to become completely silent and to listen attentively so that you may all pray together. Remind them that in order to listen well, we first become completely silent. Ask them to stand, as they do during the reading of the gospel. Say the following words that Jesus once spoke to his friends, pausing after each sentence for the children to repeat it. "Happy are those who listen to my words. Happy are those who do what my words say. You are my friends, if you do what I do."

Close the session by singing once more Song 4 on the record.

Reminder
Attendance Records Fill in the attendance record for each child.

☼ If time allows, introduce the children to the fourth celebration. Use the material on pages 31–32 of the *Celebrations* book.

Complementary Activities

☼ Show a film or tell a story. The following films and books, among others, will be useful with this theme.

Films
Corral. Contemporary Films/McGraw-Hill. 11 min., b&w.
I Like Presents. Roa Films. 25 min., color.
Moonbird. Radim Films. 10 min., color.
Play Streets. Sterling Movies. 12 min., color.

Books for Storytelling
Brown, Margaret Wise. *City Noisy Book.* New York: Harper and Row, 1976; $1.95 (paper).

Elkin, Benjamin. *The Loudest Noise in the World*. New York: Viking Press, 1954; $6.95.

Ets, Marie Hall. *In the Forest*. Viking Press, 1970; $.75.

———. *Just Me*. Viking Press, 1970; $.75.

———. *Play with Me*. Viking Press, 1970; $.95.

Lane, Carolyn. *The Voices of Greenwillow Pond*. Boston: Houghton Mifflin, 1972; $4.95.

L'Engle, Madeleine. *A Circle of Quiet*. New York: Fawcett World, 1975; $1.50.

Piatti, Celestino. *The Happy Owls*. Atheneum, 1964; $5.95.

Rand, Ann and Paul. *Listen, Listen*. New York: Harcourt Brace Jovanovich, 1970; $4.95.

Showers, Paul. *The Listening Walk*. New York: Thomas Y. Crowell, 1961; $4.50.

Sicotte, Virginia. *A Riot of Quiet*. New York: Holt, Rinehart & Winston, 1969; $2.95.

☼ Consider the suggestions given below for activities for the home session.

Home Session

Aim   To teach your child to listen attentively to God's Word proclaimed in the Liturgy of the Word and to act upon it

Review   Ask your child to tell you about the work he or she did on pages 26 and 27 of the "golden book." Help him or her recall what was discussed in class about listening to people and about the Bible. Review what your child has learned about the Bible.

The New Testament tells us about Jesus.   Show your child the New Testament. Tell him or her it was written by Jesus' close friends. They wanted everyone to know about Jesus—what he says and what he does for people.

In the New Testament we read about the many things Jesus did for his friends: he helped people who were poor, ill, and very sad; people who had no one to help them; people who wanted to know how much God, our heavenly Father, loves us and how they could love him more.

In the New Testament we also read what Jesus tells us about the joy of God's kingdom and how we should prepare for it here on earth. Jesus tells us that when we bring joy and love and peace to people who live with us on earth, we prepare for heaven, and that the kingdom of heaven will be given to us as our great reward. Jesus says to us, "Happy are those who make peace. Happy are those who comfort others, for the kingdom of heaven is theirs."

Explain to your child that when we see people who love one another, who care for one another, then we may say that we can look at Jesus, who works through them. These people have taken the time to see how Jesus acted with people and they act in the same manner. They listen to the words of Jesus. They keep Jesus' words in their heart and do what his words tell them to do. Ask your child what he or she remembers about the importance of listening to people we love. Then tell him or her that we should also listen to Jesus. Jesus tells us, "You shall be happy if you do as I do" and "You shall be happy if you listen to my words and do what they say."

Many people listen to Jesus.

Share with your child a few examples of your own efforts, in specific situations, to do what Jesus asks. Help your child discover in his or her own life how he or she has tried to put into practice some of Jesus' words.

To help your child gain some insight into the meaning of the Liturgy of the Word, explain that every week God invites us to listen to his Word at Mass. Point out some of the specific acts in the eucharistic celebrations in your parish that physically emphasize the liturgy as God's Word. For example, it may be within your child's experience to see the Bible being carried to the altar by the reader during the Entrance Procession, or to see the Bible being placed on the lectern between lighted candles to remind us that the Lord is with us through his Word.

Liturgical Emphasis

The Readings Tell your child that after we have asked God's forgiveness and one another's forgiveness at Mass and have said or sung words of praise to God, the reader comes to the lectern. Everyone is seated so

63

that we can listen well. We become very still. The reader reads from the Bible. We look at the reader and listen carefully to every word he or she says. Then we thank God for his Word.

Meditation Explain that the Word of God needs to reach deep into our mind and into our heart. That is why we say or sing a meditation psalm when the reader has completed the readings. You might read with your child "Your Words, O Lord," on page 28 of the "golden book."

Point out that the celebrant then rises and comes to the lectern. We all rise, too, and often we sing an Alleluia to welcome Jesus, who is with us when his words are read to us. You might sing together an Alleluia that your child knows or one that is often sung in your parish. Then sing Song 4 on the record *We Celebrate the Eucharist.*

The Gospel Explain that the word *gospel* comes from *god-spel*, which means "good news." The Lord speaks to us through the gospel. At Mass we stand to listen to his words.

Activities **Reading** Read together the text on pages 28 and 30 of your child's book to bring into clearer focus what you have considered about the Liturgy of the Word.

Writing Help your child remember some of Jesus' words, and give him or her crayons to write them in the space provided on page 30.

Drawing Have your child draw a picture of what he or she sees and does when we listen to God's Word in God's house.

Interpretation When your child has completed the drawing, ask him or her to show it to you and tell you about it. As always, use specific questions. For example, "Where are we? Who is that? What is he (she) doing? What are these people doing? Where are you? What are you doing?"

Prayer Ask your child to repeat the following prayer after you, sentence by sentence. "Lord, open my ears to your words so that I can hear them. Lord, open my heart to your words so that I can love them. Lord, open my eyes so that I can see you in people. Lord, give me your strength to do what your words tell me to do. Here I am, Lord. Speak to me."

Reminder

64 Please sign your child's book on pages 27 and 31.

Storytelling You might select one or more of the books listed on pages 61–62, above, to read with your child during the week. Through your interchange of ideas, you might help your child understand more fully the role of listening in his or her life.

Bible Reading Encourage your child to read with you a few words from the gospel booklet he or she received at the celebration. This could be an ideal evening prayer.

Favorite Story Together with your child, make a list of his or her favorite stories. Invite the child to choose one to listen to now. Then discuss what it was about hearing this story that makes it one for retelling.

Bible Stories Proceed as above, but with the Bible stories your child recalls.

Favorite Sound Talk about your favorite sound and why you like it. Then invite your child to do the same.

Whispering Whisper something in someone's ear. Let it go around the whole family. See if the last thing heard was the first thing said.

The Eucharist:
It's About Caring

For Saint Paul, the Church community, the family of God, is a community of mutual service in which each member serves the others, in which each part is equally concerned for the whole and all its parts. In Paul's description of the body of Christ (1 Corinthians 12:4-11), his first concern is not so much who possesses what gift, who has what to offer, but that each person offer what he or she has, and that all work together for the common good.

But Paul was not a visionary without roots, a dreamer divorced from reality. His vision is a beautiful reflection on the essential meaning of Jesus Christ. Jesus Christ is the identification of God with humanity—in a word, of the lover with the beloved. God *cares* for us. This is the Incarnation. As in every relationship of love, the depth of identification is a measure of the depth of the love. Christ achieved a degree of identification with us that staggers our imagination and challenges the human spirit. He so shared our human condition, he was so much at one with us in our situation, that he could tell his disciples, "He who welcomes you welcomes me" (Matthew 10:40). He could say to Paul, "Saul, Saul, why do you persecute me?" (Acts 9:4). He could tell each person who would follow him, "As often as you did it for one of my least brothers, you did it for me" (Matthew 25:40).

INTRODUCTION TO THE THEME

67

The love that Christ's identification with us signifies calls for a response as all love does. It seeks to evoke an identification on our part with him. And it is *his* identification with *us* that makes that response possible. Christ has not departed from our midst. He is not simply an historical memory, to be thought of on occasion. He is present to us in many ways as he promised—not the least of which is in our brothers and sisters.

The fact that he has so identified himself with each of us and with all of us together offers us the opportunity of finding him in one another. By identifying with one another, we respond to Christ's offer of love. In the service of others, we identify in our turn with Christ. Is there any other way to understand this appeal of St. John's to Christians? "Beloved, if God has loved us so, we must have the same love for one another" (1 John 4:11).

The Christian community is a community of people because they are aware of God's identification in love with each one of them and all of them together. They respond to his love in their service to one another. Each offers what he or she has, who he or she is, to the others, and thus serves the good of all. Within the Christian community, the service of the Christian to others builds up the Church, strengthens God's family, so that together they are a sign to the world of the love of God. Within the world community, the service of Christians to others strengthens the whole human family and is a sign to each of us that God has identified himself with every person, that God loves every person as an individual.

Every act of service, every gesture of caring that we Christians manifest toward others is a sign of the identification of God with all humankind.

Nowhere does the fact that God cares for us become more evident than in our Christian celebration of the Eucharist. In the eucharistic celebration, we nourish the life that is ours through God's love made visible in baptism. We celebrate the reality that ours is a shared life, and we strengthen the unity we have. We express our desire to share our life with others, and we recognize we have not done so to the full. We listen to God's Word of love for us, which tells of his care for us.

Also in the celebration of the Eucharist, our response to God's loving care for us becomes evident through our care for one another. In the Prayer of the Faithful, we declare in effect that the community to which we belong is not turned in on itself but is turned toward service to others. We show that the life we celebrate is truly to be shared. We give evidence of truly having listened to God's Word of love. In the Prayer of the Faithful, we show that we care.

We pray for the whole Church, that this community may truly become a sign of the interrelatedness of life in Jesus Christ. We pray, for example, for civil authorities, for those oppressed by various needs, and for the salvation of the world, that every member of the human family may become aware that someone cares for him or her.

All the richness of God's care converges in the Eucharist. In this Christian celebration, we become aware through word and symbol of how much God loves us, of how deeply he has identified himself with us. The Prayer of the Faithful, our prayerful concern for one another, expresses our response to God's love.

Group Session

To help the children become attentive to the needs of others and to discover ways to respond concretely to those needs

Aim

Greet the children with special care and love. Talk with them about their work on page 29 of their book.

Review

Ask the children to open their book to pages 32 and 33. Discuss the pictures with them. Ask them to describe what the pictures tell them about people who care for others and about people who are in need of love, care, and help. (Stress the invisible needs expressed in the pictures as much as the material needs.) You might use questions such as the following to aid in the discussion.

Many people care for us.

"What may have happened to the girl in the first picture? What is her father doing? How do you think she feels about her father? What is happening in the next picture? How do you think the girl feels because her friends have come to visit her? How do you feel when your friends share things with you?

"Let's look at the pictures of the girl and the baby. Do you think the girl is taking good care of the baby? How can you tell? Do you ever care for a little brother or sister? How do you feel when you can make people happy because you care for them? Look at the boy in the last picture. Why do you think he seems so happy? Who do you think loves him and cares for him? Do you have a grandmother or a grandfather who loves and cares for you? How can you show them that you love them too?"

Relate the experiences presented through the pictures to simple daily situations that are relevant to the children's lives and to which they can react. Conclude by pointing out that our parents, teachers, and friends surround us with love and care. Without them we cannot live.

We also care for people. Let the children tell you how they would try to give joy and help to some of the people in the pictures. Once again, help the children realize that people sometimes have as great a need for love, affection, and friendship as they do for material goods. Our presence, our kindness, a smile, a visit, a postcard are valued by others because they are expressions of our love and caring.

Activities **Reading**   Ask the children to open their book to page 34. Call upon children to read one paragraph each; then ask them all to think for a few minutes about how they would answer the questions raised.

Note—Asking a young child to read aloud in a group of relative strangers can be a sensitive matter. As a general rule invite the whole group to read aloud, with you leading them. If, as we here suggest, you do invite individuals to read, be sure they are children who will read solo without being unduly uncomfortable. This is not an exercise in language arts but a reflective activity for a sacramental initiation.

Writing   Distribute crayons or felt-tipped pens, and have each child fill in the spaces with the names of people to whom he or she can bring joy and happiness by caring for them.

Drawing   Ask the children to illustrate, on page 35 of their book, the theme of the lesson on caring. They might draw a picture of people who need their love and care. They might make a collage with pictures and headlines cut from magazines and newspapers. Some children might prefer to write a story.

Interpretation   As soon as a child has finished an illustration, ask him or her to come to you to show you the work and tell you about it. Help each child express his or her thoughts by asking specific questions, such as, "Who is this? Why does he (she) look unhappy? What can we do for him (her)? This person looks happy. Why? Who cares for him (her)? Why do you think the person cares?"

Writing   Invite the children to write on a card the name of a person they can help or who is in need of their care, and their petition for that person. Direct them also to write their own name on their card, for the children will be invited at the next celebration to offer their cards to the celebrant. If a child is unable to write, ask him or her to dictate the petition to you as you write it down.

Singing   Teach the children a simple melody for "Lord, Have Mercy," and sing it with them several times so that they can sing it easily. Then sing with them Song 5 on the record *We Celebrate the Eucharist.*

Prayer   Explain that you would like each child to pray for the particular person he or she has named on the card, with all the children singing "Lord, Have Mercy" after each petition. Ask them to become very still. Introduce the prayer in the following manner. "Lord, we are here before you to pray for people who need us. Lord, listen to the prayers of your children."

Then invite each child to pray the petition from his or her card. Follow each petition by singing together the invocation. Conclude by praying, "Lord, you give us people who care for us and who love us. Give us your Spirit of love so that we may always care for people who need our love and prayers."

Reminders
Be sure to collect the petition cards before the children leave. The cards are to be distributed to the children before the next celebration. The children will present their petition cards to the celebrant during the Offertory Procession.

Attendance Records   Fill in the attendance record for each child.

☼ Children in WE CELEBRATE THE EUCHARIST in Saint Louis wrote to senior citizens, one on one, asking them to pray for the writer of   *Complementary Activities* the letter, who would soon be making his or her First Communion. Each letter also extended an invitation to the older person to attend the celebration on the theme of Caring. When the time came for the celebration, each child welcomed his or her invitee, and afterwards invited the senior citizen to join in the remaining celebrations as well—including, especially, the First Communion celebration itself. Throughout, the point was made clear that the *senior citizen was being asked to care for the candidate* in two ways—by praying for, and by celebrating with, him or her. You may wish to do this with your group.

✿ You may wish to introduce the children to the fifth celebration if you have time. Follow the directions on page 43 of *Celebrations*.

✿ Show a film or tell a story.

Films
Buttercup. TeleKETICS. 11 min., color.
Hands: Not for a Million. St. Francis Productions. 5 min., color.
Here Is a Woman. St. Francis Productions. 5 min., color.
I Have to Face Things for Myself. Roa Films. 25 min., color.
The Red Balloon. Brandon Films. 34 min., color.
Rich Cat, Poor Cat. McGraw-Hill Films. 8 min., color.
A Very Special Day. Universal Education & Visual Arts. 19 min., color.
The Stray. TeleKETICS. 14 min., color.

Books for Storytelling
Alexander, Martha G. *Nobody Asked Me If I Wanted a Baby Sister*. New York: Dial, 1971; $3.50.
Byars, Betsy. *Go and Hush the Baby*. New York: Viking Press, 1971; $3.37.
Flack, Marjorie. *Ask Mr. Bear*. New York: Macmillan, 1958; $3.95. Paper (1971), $1.25.
———. *Wait for William*. Boston: Houghton Mifflin, n.d.; $6.95.
Harrison, Richard, and Albert Adler. *Children's Answers to Everything*. New York: Simon & Schuster, 1969; $2.00.
Hoban, Russell. *Best Friends for Frances*. New York: Harper and Row, 1969; $3.95. Paper (1976), $1.95.

Kraus, Robert. *Whose Mouse Are You?* New York: Macmillan, 1970; $5.95. Paper (1972), $1.25.

Lionni, Leo. *Tico and the Golden Wings.* New York: Pantheon, 1964; $4.95. Paper, $1.25.

Slobodkin, Louis. *One Is Good but Two Are Better.* New York: Vanguard, 1956; $4.95.

Udry, Janice May. *What Mary Jo Shared.* Chicago: Albert Whitman, 1968; $4.50.

☼ You might consider using some of the activities recommended below for the home session.

Home Session

To help your child realize that in helping others the Spirit of Jesus is present in his or her life

Aim

Ask your child to tell you about the work completed in the "golden book," pages 34 and 35, on the theme of caring for people. Discuss the work and then ask your child to consider how, through one concrete action this week, he or she might care for someone he or she knows. What is of the greatest importance here is your child's own personal response.

Review

Ask your child to comment on the pictures introducing the theme of caring, pages 32 and 33. Together, share experiences of loving and caring for others. Consider how a parent cares for the welfare of his or her family, how a teacher cares for the children in his or her classroom, how a nurse, a sanitation worker, a police officer, a baker care for people's needs. Help your child recognize that because so many people care for others, you can have a happy family and a happy neighborhood.

People need people.

Using the pictures on pages 32 and 33 once more, point out that some children do not have all the people they need to take care of them. Ask your child how he or she thinks the children in the pictures might feel if there was no one to comfort them, no friends to bring cheer, no sister to entertain the baby, no grandfather to take interest in a project.

Then reflect on other situations. For example, there are children who have no teachers to teach them; children who have no doctors or nurses to heal them. There are children whose parents are unable to work for them because they are ill or cannot find a job; children who have no mother or father, no friends, no toys, or even enough to eat.

I can care for people.

You, more than anyone, know of people to whom your child can bring joy and happiness—perhaps a classmate who has been confined to bed for a time and has been forgotten by playmates; perhaps a grandparent who would love your child's company; perhaps a child who has been rejected by the children of the neighborhood or on the playground and who needs a friend. Discuss one or two people within your child's experience and environment to whom he or she can bring love and joy.

Ask your child to listen to what Jesus tells us about caring for one another. Relate the following adaptation of Matthew 25: 31-40.

"One day Jesus gave his friends a very important message. He said that when he came back on the last day he would gather before him the people of the whole world, and he would say to many of them, 'Come now, enter into the kingdom of heaven, which I have prepared for you. And this is why you shall receive the joy of heaven: When I was hungry, you fed me. When I was thirsty, you gave me drink. When I was a stranger, you welcomed me in your home. When I had no clothes to wear, you clothed me. When I was sick and lonely, you visited me.' Then Jesus' friends asked him, 'Lord, when did we do all these things for you? We cannot remember.' Jesus answered, 'I tell you indeed, whenever you cared for and loved the least of your brothers and sisters, you did it for me.' "

There is joy in caring for others.

Point out that when we care for someone our joy will be great in heaven; but even now whenever we care and do something for a person, it can also be like heaven within our hearts.

Some people say that it hurts to share time and joy with others. This is not really true. Whenever we share something with someone who needs us, we see the joy on that person's face and at the same moment the Spirit of Jesus fills our heart with happiness. Relate an incident from your own experience in which you saw how happy someone became because of your help and how the person's happiness filled your own heart with joy.

The Prayer of the Faithful Explain to your child that whenever we celebrate the Eucharist, we pray for those who need our love and care. Read the text on page 36 of your child's book. The Prayer of the Faithful reminds us of the many people who have no one to care for them and who need our prayers. It also names people who care for us and for whom we should pray.

Liturgical Emphasis

Reading Turn to page 38 of the "golden book." Read together Jesus' words. Help your child reflect on each sentence. To prevent Jesus' words from remaining abstract to your child, you might ask him or her to recall incidents from personal experience—for example, when he or she made up after a quarrel, shared something with others, tried to comfort someone—incidents that were rewarding experiences and concrete reflections of Jesus' words.

Activities

Writing Help your child fill in the spaces on page 38 with names of people who put into practice the words of Jesus.

Turn to page 39. Read the sentence at the top of the page. Speak briefly of the many needs you have discussed together. Then help your child fill in the spaces with names of people he or she wishes to care about and pray for.

Prayer Using the names of the people your child has suggested, compose a litany with him or her and pray it together. After your child names each person and perhaps gives a reason for wishing to pray for the person, you might respond, "Lord, hear our prayer."

Reminder

Please sign your child's book on pages 35 and 39.

Storytelling We suggest that during the week you read with your child one of the stories recommended on pages 72–73 of this guide.

Get-Well Card Make a get-well card for someone in particular. Send it to that person (or, better, take it to him or her).

Caretaker Collage In the center of a large sheet of paper or cardboard, paste a picture of your family. Then, around the picture, paste or draw pictures of the many people who in some way take care of you—grocers, teachers, sanitation workers, clergy, nurses, for example. Take as many days as you need to complete your work. The whole family can help.

Complementary Activities

The Eucharist:

It's About Giving Thanks for Creation

The age-old Christian vision is that all of creation has been given to human beings by a loving God so that they might extend their mastery over it.

From the first pages of Scripture, this vision is set in relief. The accounts of creation in Genesis are poetic, not scientific. They represent a testimony of faith; they are not history in the modern sense of the word. The writers' intention was to express their awareness that all creation is a manifestation of God *for us,* an expression of God's concern *for us.* Central to their vision was the conviction that the human race stood at the summit of creation, that it was intended to be both the centerpiece of God's creation and master of it.

INTRODUCTION TO THE THEME

The dignity and the power with which God has invested humanity and the responsibility that flows from this grace are unmistakably expressed in this psalm:

> *You have made him little less than the angels,*
> *and crowned him with glory and honor.*
> *You have given him rule over the works*
> *of your hands,*
> *putting all things under his feet....*
> *O Lord, our Lord,*
> *how glorious is your name over all*
> *the earth! (8:6-7, 10).*

In addition to this responsibility for caring for creation, Scripture also describes our proper response to God's concern and love as one of thankful praise for creation.

That we should make such a response should not be altogether surprising. People who really give and receive love in the day-to-day course of life need at times to express themselves in a word or gesture of love-response. A lover's kiss, a child's smile, joyful voices raised in song— each shows that we are essentially expressive beings, who must in some way openly acknowledge what we feel, what we are, what has been done for us.

All of creation is a sign of God's concern. It is all truly *for us*. In the Christian vision, it is correctly seen as God's gift to us, who are the summit of creation itself. Creation alone, however, does not fully reveal God's concern for us. Above all else, God has shown himself to be truly for us through his Son, Jesus. Through Jesus and in Jesus, people are not only liberated from servitude to this physical world but also set free from slavery to themselves. It is the selfless love of God for us, manifested in creation, and especially in Jesus Christ, that alone can free us from selfishness, from imprisonment in ourselves. It is this love that Christians gratefully acknowledge.

The Christian is one who daily gives and receives love. Thus he or she must respond to this love openly in thankful praise. This response is the foundation of the Eucharist. The thanksgiving aspect of the eucharistic celebration was originally expressed by Christ and the early community in the words of a grace, a blessing, at meals. When this Christian celebration became separated from the context of a meal in the second century, this element of thanksgiving, which had always been central, was made even more explicit.

The basic structure of the Mass became the prayer of thanksgiving pronounced over the gifts and the preparation of the gifts. Yet despite the change in structure, the object of thanksgiving remained the same: the wonderful works of God for humanity.

After the Prayer of the Faithful, the gifts are brought forward to the celebrant. It is becoming the custom to bring forward money and other gifts that have been collected for the Church and the poor at the same time the bread and wine are brought forward. This rite is a forceful expression of gratitude for the goods of the earth in which we share.

The celebrant accepts the bread and wine in our name with grateful acknowledgment of the Creator. In preparing the gifts, he acknowledges in a prayer that these elements, which in this celebration will become symbols of God's liberating love in Jesus Christ, are first of all signs to us of his presence in the universe. This part of the celebration is essentially a thanksgiving for the gifts of creation, an acknowledgment of the gift to us of the material universe. The celebrant offers in return its first fruits, not as if God needed them, but as signs of our thankfulness.

When the gifts have been prepared, the celebrant prays over them, asking God that these elements of bread and wine truly become the food and drink of our lives. At this point, we enter fully into the eucharistic mystery. If there ever was any doubt about the meaning of our coming together, it should disappear when the celebrant issues his resounding invitation to the community, opening the great Eucharistic Prayer: "Let us give thanks to the Lord our God."

In the Preface, the celebrant gives thanks in our name for the love and concern with which God has touched his people throughout history; and in the "Holy, holy, holy," we acknowledge the universality of God's love for us. It is above all in the Eucharistic Prayer, which now begins, that we enthusiastically give thanks for the love and concern of God revealed in creation and in the Incarnation. In it, we give thanks to one who loves us at the very core of our lives.

Group Session

Aim

To help the children acknowledge the countless gifts that surround them in creation and to foster an attitude of thanksgiving to God for all these gifts

Review

Welcome each child personally. Acknowledge the work he or she has done on pages 38 and 39 of the "golden book."

The world is a beautiful gift.

Ask the children to open their book to pages 40 and 41. Ask them to look at the picture of the sunrise and the picture of the swans. Show your admiration for these pictures; then ask the children what they like most about the pictures. Ask them to name other sights that they think are very beautiful too. You might ask, "What do you think is as beautiful as the sunrise? What are some of your favorite things? What is your favorite animal? Why is it your favorite?"

God is the Creator of the world.

Point out to the children that often when you see the great beauty in the world and the wonderful things there are to enjoy, you ask yourself, "Who is so beautiful as to have made such a beautiful world? Who is this beautiful world for?" Then explain that God loves us so much that he gives us this world for everyone to enjoy.

People are very special gifts.

Ask the children to look at the picture of the boy on page 41. Comment on how happy he appears to be. Then ask them why they think the boy appears to be so happy. Help them relate their explanations ultimately to the goodness, love, and generosity of people who love them.

Talk with the children about people in their own lives who are "gifts" to them. Help them recognize more fully that so much of the joy, comfort, and encouragement they experience is brought to them by others.

Draw the children's attention to the picture of the construction workers on page 40 of their book. Encourage them to describe what the picture says to them. You might ask questions such as these: "What do you think these people are making? Have you ever seen anyone working so high up? How do these people help many other people?" Talk about the people who contribute to the well-being of others by using their special skills and talents. Ask the children to name some of the people who directly help others through their work and to describe how they help others.

Explain to the children that after God made the earth, he made people to live on the earth. Present God's creation of people as an act of love, of God's wanting to share his life and love with everyone. Point out that God knows every person by name, he loves every person, and cares about every person. God gives every person special skills and talents.

God is the Creator of people.

Reading Ask the children to turn to page 42 of their book. Ask individuals to read aloud one verse each of the prayer. Or lead the group in reading the whole prayer together.

Activities

Singing You might sing with the children Song 6 or Song 7 on the record *We Celebrate the Eucharist.*

Drawing Ask each child to make an Offertory card depicting his or her favorite people and things. Provide the children with colored paper, felt-tipped pens or crayons, scissors, tape, colorful pictures cut from magazines, and, if possible, some shells, feathers, sand, and glitter.

After the children have designed their cards, ask them to print on the cards their name and a short thank-you note to God.

As a separate activity, ask the children to start their drawing on page 43 of their book. This activity may be completed at home if there is not sufficient time in class.

Interpretation After each child has completed an Offertory card, speak with him or her about it. Compliment the child on the number and variety of gifts included. Then add, "Tell me more about the gifts you have pictured here. Which ones are very special to you? Which ones do you enjoy every day? Tell me about this gift. It tells me that someone really cares about you. How does it make you feel?"

Gesture Teach the children the thanksgiving gesture of the Eucharistic Prayer. Slowly raise your hands and arms in a gesture of thanksgiving. Ask the children to make the gesture; then all sing together a Eucharistic Acclamation.

Prayer Ask the children to stand and give thanks with hands and voice to God our Father, who gives us so many gifts. Invite them to express why they want to give thanks to God. They might relate their reply to what they have depicted on their Offertory cards. After each child's statement, ask all to sing or say, "We Give You Thanks, O God Our Father." You might close this thanksgiving litany by asking the children to hold up their Offertory cards as they sing Song 6 or Song 7 on the record.

Reminders

Be sure to collect the Offertory cards. These cards are to be distributed to the children before the next celebration. The children will present them to the celebrant during the Offertory Procession.

Attendance Records Fill in the attendance record for each child.

Complementary Activities

☼ If time allows, prepare the sixth celebration by using pages 55–56 of the *Celebrations* book. Prepare the dialogue at the bottom of page 58 of the same book (the dialogue that introduces the Preface).

☼ Show a film or tell a story to point up the meaning of Theme 6.

Films

Creation. Roa Films. 5 min., color.
God's Grandeur. TeleKETICS. 3½ min., color.
Hailstones and Halibut Bones. Sterling Movies. 6 min., color.
Sky. Contemporary Films/McGraw-Hill. 9 min., color.
Snowy Day. Weston Woods Studios. 6 min., color.
Time of Wonder. Weston Woods Studios. 13 min., color.

Books for Storytelling

Clark, Ann N. *In My Mother's House.* New York: Viking Press, 1941; $5.95. Paper (1972), $1.50.
Ets, Marie Hall. *Gilberto and the Wind.* New York: Viking Press, 1963; $4.95. (Also available in Spanish.) Paper (1969), $.95.

Francoise. *Thank-You Book.* New York: Scribner, 1947; $6.95.

Goddard, Carrie Lou. *Isn't It a Wonder!* Nashville: Abingdon, 1977; $4.25.

Krauss, Ruth. *A Hole Is to Dig.* New York: Harper and Row, 1952; $2.95.

Lemke, Horst. *Places and Faces.* Scroll Press, 1971; $3.95.

The Marvels of Animal Behavior. Washington, D.C.: National Geographic Society, 1972; $9.80.

☼ Consider some of the activities listed below for the home session.

Home Session

To reveal to your child that the greatest gift among all gifts bestowed on us by God is his only Son, Jesus

Aim

Read with your child The Prayer of Saint Francis, page 42 of the "golden book." You might ask him or her to complete the drawing on page 43 if it is not already finished. Help your child describe how each gift depicted there has special meaning and value in his or her everyday life.

Review

Ask your child to turn back to the pictures on pages 40 and 41. Comment on the variety of the beauty and goodness that exists in the world. Explain that all the world is a gift from God. He loves us so much that he made the world for us. You might read to your child the account of creation in Chapter 1 of the Book of Genesis.

The world is a gift from God.

Discuss some of the ways by which human beings build a better world. You might start by considering the first picture on page 40. Then explain that God gives us a body and a mind so that we can do many remarkable things. He gives us skills and talents. He gives us the ability to enjoy life, to laugh, to have friends, and to be a friend to others. God gives us the power to love one another.

Humanity is the masterpiece of God's creation.

God loves us so much that he gives us his Son, Jesus. Reveal to your child that the greatest of God's gifts to us is the gift of his Son, Jesus. Through Jesus we become children of God, we receive a new life. Through Jesus we shall live forever in a world even more beautiful than this world with people who will always love one another. Through Jesus we shall receive the gift of heaven, a new life of love, of beauty and joy that shall never end. A friend of God's tells us, "God loves us so much that he gives us his only Son, Jesus" (adapted from 1 John 4:9).

Liturgical Emphasis   **Offertory Procession and Song** Discuss what was done at the celebration during the Offertory Procession. If the children brought their Offertory cards to the altar, you might discuss this gesture with your child. Gifts are brought to the altar because we know that everything we have is a gift from God. We want to say "Thank you" to God for all he gives us. As we offer our gifts to God during the Offertory Procession, we sing a song. Sing with your child Song 6 or Song 7 on the record *We Celebrate the Eucharist,* or another song of offering.

Thanksgiving Prayer Discuss the picture on page 45. Observe the gesture made by the celebrant as he invites us to join him in a prayer of thanksgiving shortly after the Offertory Procession. Review the many gifts we want to thank God for: the beauty of creation, the greatness and power of humanity, the love of people who surround us, the love of God in sending us his Son, Jesus.

Activities   **Reading** Read together the text of the Eucharistic Prayer for Masses with Children, page 44 of the "golden book." Then read or sing together the acclamation "Holy, holy, holy" on the same page. Then read page 46 together.

Writing Ask your child to write a prayer of thanksgiving in the space provided on page 46. It may be dictated if your child prefers.

Drawing Turn to page 47. Read the words taken from Saint John's gospel. Then ask your child to decorate the page to express what God's sending us Jesus means to him or her.

Discuss some of the gifts for which we can give thanks to the Lord daily; for example, a beautiful day, food, friends, a flower in the garden, the songs of birds, the moon. Help your child pray a short prayer of thanksgiving.

Singing   You could bring this home session to an end by singing together Song 6 or Song 7 on the record *We Celebrate the Eucharist.*

Reminder
Please sign your child's book on pages 43 and 47.

Storytelling   You might read to your child one of the stories suggested on pages 82–83 of this guide and then discuss it with him or her in terms of the child's own gifts from God.

Complementary Activities

Favorite Things   List your "favorite things in creation," in the manner of the song "My Favorite Things."

Walk   On a nice day take a walk through a park or a wildlife sanctuary. Express wonder before God's marvellous creation.

Geology   Take a family outing to a place where there are interesting rocks. Collect some, and place them in a bed of sand for a mini-Zen garden. Or draw a large picture of the earth cut in two (consult an encyclopedia) and use some clay to attach some of your rocks to it.

Seashore   A few hours of combing a beach or riverbank together should provide enough material to keep you in wonder for a month.

The Eucharist:

It's About Giving Thanks for New Life

In the course of human development, we often experience "dying" in order to grow and to live more fully. Death is present to some degree in everything that diminishes life in our human experience—in pain, suffering, alienation, frustration. Death manifests itself in prejudice, bigotry, hatred, violence—in everything that poses an obstacle to growth, development, and dignity. Whatever in our experience is dehumanizing, whatever is hostile to life, is death in a minor form.

Leaving behind the former self, and taking up the new self, in passing from childhood to adolescence (or from adolescence to adulthood) is a familiar example of the real, though perhaps at times unconscious, dying that is involved in human development.

And certainly a kind of dying takes place when two people decide to give up some of their independence and self-consideration as individuals in order to enter the life of marriage and parenthood. The same "dying" is at work in the decision to enter religious life or ministry.

INTRODUCTION TO THE THEME

87

At times the death we encounter is a lessening of life and an obstacle to growth. At other times, the dying we experience is in order that we may grow. In both cases, however, there is a force that prevents the dying from becoming complete, and also enables growth to take place no matter how painful or difficult. That force is love. Love alone in its various manifestations is capable of overcoming death. Love alone is able to offer a person the security needed in order to give up the old life and take on the new. Love is the most powerful life-giving force we know.

Nowhere is the reality of love as the most powerful life-giving force more obvious than in the life of Jesus Christ. In him we encounter God's love for us in a form so absolute that it is capable of overcoming death in *all* its forms. And so it offers the possibility of growth to the fulness of life. We Christians believe that in Jesus Christ, God delivers us from sin, which is, after all, another form of death.

Our celebration of the Eucharist is an acknowledgment of our gratitude to God for what he has done for us, but especially for having freed us from death.

It is above all in the Eucharistic Prayer that we acknowledge in thankful praise the events by which we have all been saved and, most of all, the death and resurrection of Jesus Christ. As at the first Eucharist, the elements of bread and wine are transformed by the creative word of Jesus Christ, and they become his body and blood. In the context of the Eucharistic Prayer, these elements receive from Christ a new and deeper meaning and so serve to open us out onto Jesus Christ. They make Christ really present to us in a sacramental manner, Christ who is already present to us in the liturgical assembly, in the celebrant in liturgical service, in the ministry of the Word, and in all the other sacraments.

The words of consecration that the celebrant pronounces in this prayer of thanksgiving are not a magic formula, but rather an essential part of our prayer. These words, and the words just before them, tell us something about Christ's purpose in making himself present in this way and something about the kind of presence it is.

It becomes evident both in word and in gesture that Christ is really present to us in the bread and in the wine *to offer himself to us* and *to be taken by us,* so that he may be intimately present in each of our hearts and in the heart of the whole community of believers. Christ is not present "just to be there." He is present to give himself to us and to be accepted by us so that he may truly live in us and we in him.

The words of consecration themselves tell us something more of the manner or character of his presence. They tell us that he is present to us in a sacrificial way. They tell us that we are offered Christ's body, which has been "given up for us," and his blood, which has been "shed for us." It is this self-giving, real presence of Christ that gives the Eucharist its character of sacrifice. It is this self-giving of Christ, too, that we commemorate, and in which we participate, when we make the sacrifice of the Eucharist our own.

The Memorial Acclamation that follows the words of consecration is, in a sense, a summary of the whole of the Eucharistic Prayer. Also, it is a joyous expression of our belief that God *has* saved us in Jesus Christ and especially that this salvation touches us in a real and visible manner in this Eucharist.

The prayer itself closes with the great Amen, the community's expression of faith. Here we voice our Yes to Christ who has made himself present to us, and we express our desire to open ourselves to his saving presence.

Human experience shows us that death is inevitable, that it is a reality every person must encounter. At the same time, it shows us that death is not simply an ultimate reality, one that lies in the future, but a real force at work in the here and now of our lives. Jesus Christ has shown us that death is not the ultimate reality at all; it is life, not death, that has the final say. And in the Eucharist we give thanks that in Christ, God's love has overcome death in all its forms. We give thanks for life itself.

Group Session

Aim To help the children discover that people who love one another give of themselves for others through daily actions

Review   Welcome each child. Look at his or her drawing on page 43 of the "golden book." Commend each child on his or her particular insights into the theme of creation.

People who love us share their life and love with us. Discuss with the children the many people who share their life every day. Help them acknowledge the people who so generously give of themselves for the children's happiness and whose love and concern for them is so necessary for their well-being. Encourage the children to think first of the people closest to them: their parents or guardians, brothers and sisters, grandparents, playmates, neighbors. Then extend the discussion to the many members of the community who help them and care for them: their teachers, the bus driver, the school crossing guard, the mail carrier, and neighborhood program leaders.

We want to be with people who love us.   Help the children reflect on how they like to be with people who love them and provide for their needs. Consider how they need the presence of others, their understanding, friendship, help, and comfort. For example, when they return home after school, they love to see their mother and father and tell them all about their day at school. When they are ill, they are "hungry" to have their mother or father come into their room and spend some time with them. They long for a brother, sister, or friend to come to visit them and tell them what happened at school.

Activities   **Picture Discussion**   Have the children open their book to pages 48 and 49. Ask them what the pictures tell them about people who give of themselves for others. You might use these guidelines:

"Look at the little boy who is ill. What is his mother doing? Do you think he likes his mother to be close by? Did you ever have to stay in bed because you were ill? Were you happy to have someone stay in your room with you? Why do you think someone did this for you?

"The next picture is quite different, isn't it? Everyone looks well and happy. What are they doing? What are some fun things you do with your family? Why, do you think, do they all look so happy?

"Look at the next picture. These children may be a brother and a sister or they may be good friends. What are they doing? What are some of your favorite games? Is it much fun to play a game alone? What games are most fun to play? Why?

90

"Now look at the last picture, showing the many golden crosses. What does this picture say to you? You will learn more about what these crosses mean at the next celebration."

Reading   Ask the children to turn the page. Ask several children to read a sentence each to the group.

Writing   Ask the children to fill in the spaces on page 50 of their book. Assist any children in their work if they need help. Move among the children as they work. Encourage them to think about their answers.

Drawing   Invite each child to show, by drawing or pasting pictures, people sharing their life and love with others.

Interpretation   As each child completes this work, invite him or her to show it to you and tell you about it. Use specific questions such as these to help the children express their thoughts: "Who is this person? Tell me more abouut him (her). How does he (she) share his (her) life with others? What about *this* person? Why is he (she) in your picture? How do the people in your picture make you feel?"

Singing   Teach Song 8 on the record *We Celebrate the Eucharist*. Teach the Memorial Acclamation "Christ has died," or another. Teach a Great Amen ("Amen, Amen, Amen"). Always discuss the meaning of the words of any songs you may choose to teach. For instance, explain to the children that whenever we put our trust in others or share our life with others, we are telling them Yes. In God's house, we use a special word to tell God Yes. We say or sing Amen.

Prayer   Teach the children the response "We give you thanks, O God our Father." Then invite them to stand and pray the following litany of thanksgiving, asking them to give the response at the proper time.

"For the time, the attention, and the daily bread that our parents give to us, we give you thanks, O God our Father. For the love and care that many people show to us, we give you thanks, O God our Father. For the smiling faces and the presence of those who love us, we give you thanks, O God our Father. For those who are our 'Bread of Life,' we give you thanks, O God our Father."

Reminder
Attendance Records   After the session, fill in the attendance records.   *91*

Complementary Activities

☼ If you have additional time, you might wish to introduce the children to the celebration for Theme 7. Use page 67 of *Celebrations.*

☼ Show a film or tell a story that bears on Theme 7.

Films

Mother Tiger, Mother Tiger. TeleKETICS. 11 min., color.

The Santa Claus Suit. Contemporary Films/McGraw-Hill. 13 min., color.

The Ugly Duckling. Coronet Instructional Films. 10 min., b&w.

Books for Storytelling

Burch, Robert. *Renfroe's Christmas.* New York: Viking Press, 1968; $3.50.

Cort, Margaret. *Little Oleg.* Minneapolis, Minn.: Carolrhoda Books, 1971; $3.95.

Hoban, Russell. *A Birthday for Frances.* New York: Harper and Row, 1968; $3.95. Paper, 1976; $1.95.

Lionni, Leo. *Tico and the Golden Wings.* New York: Pantheon, 1964; $4.95. Paper, $1.25.

Minarik, Else H. *A Kiss for Little Bear.* New York: Harper and Row, 1968; $3.95.

Steptoe, John. *Stevie.* New York: Harper and Row, 1969; $5.50.

Zolotow, Charlotte. *When the Wind Stops.* New York: Harper and Row, 1975; $4.50.

☼ Consider using some of the activities recommended below for the home session.

Home Session

Aim

To help your child discover that Jesus shares a new life with us and invites us to share our life with others and that through our selfgiving, we share in the death and the resurrection of the Lord

Review

Acknowledge the work your child has done on pages 50 and 51 of the "golden book." Ask him or her to describe how the people pictured or written about share their life with others. If there are some people not included, perhaps because their presence is simply taken for granted,

92

you might mention their names and reflect with your child on how they share their life with others.

Turn to the pictures on pages 48 and 49. Consider the ordinary, everyday ways in which people share their life with others. You might point out, particularly from the second and third pictures, how children can give joy to their parents, friends, and playmates. Explain that people share their life with others because God has put his Spirit into their heart.

God gives his Spirit of love to people who share their life with others.

Select and describe an event in the life of Jesus that shows his love and concern for people and that might have particular appeal to your child. You might consider Jesus being with his mother and friends at a wedding, Jesus restoring health to a sick person, Jesus teaching his disciples, Jesus comforting a mother whose son has died, Jesus welcoming the children, Jesus giving food to the multitudes.

Jesus shared his life and love with people.

Tell your child that when Jesus had his last supper with his friends, he gave them a very important message. He said to them, "Love one another, just as I love you." Jesus told his friends that the greatest love you can have for someone is to share your life with that person. Jesus knew that it is not always easy for us to share our life with others, to help them, to be nice to them, to treat them fairly, to be happy for them when they do things better than we do. It is not always easy to say Yes to others.

Jesus teaches us to share our life with others.

Explain that Jesus knows that we need him to help us love others as he loves everyone. At the Last Supper shortly before he died and rose again, Jesus promised to be with us always and everywhere. He promised to give himself to us in a special way in the "Bread of Life." He tells us, "Whenever you receive the Bread of Life, I shall be with you and you with me." Turn to page 52 of the "golden book" and read the text. Ask your child to relate the picture on page 53 to what you have just read.

Jesus shares his life with us today.

The Sign of the Cross Turn to page 49 and explain to your child the meaning of the picture of the golden crosses. Explain that all through this theme we have considered how people share their life with others because they love them. The sign of the cross makes us think of Jesus, who gave his life for us on the cross because he loves us. On the cross Jesus said Yes to his Father for all of us. Because Jesus said Yes, God the Father raised Jesus from the dead and gave him a new life. This is why the cross of Jesus is a cross of joy, a cross of victory.

Liturgical Emphasis

93

Explain that the golden crosses stand for us. They remind us that Jesus gives us his life. He helps us say Yes to him, to his Father, and to all people.

The Great Amen Point out that at Mass we thank God our Father for sending us his Son, Jesus, through whom we share in a new and ever-lasting life. When we sing or say Amen, we mean "Yes, Jesus, we belong to you. Yes, Jesus, we share a new life with you. Yes, Jesus, we will share our life and love with others."

Sing together the Amen acclamation that was used during the celebration, or another.

Activities **Reading** Read with your child the text on page 54. Ask your child what he or she can do to say Amen to Jesus and to share his or her life with others.

Drawing Ask your child to turn to page 55 and to show, by drawing, pasting pictures, or writing a story, how Jesus shared his life and love with us by giving his life for us on the cross or by giving himself to his friends in the Bread of Life at the Last Supper.

Interpretation When your child has completed his or her picture or story, speak together about it. You might start in this way: "Tell me about your work. What does Jesus do for us today that is very much like what you have here? What does Jesus say to us? What would you like to say to Jesus?

Prayer Ask your child to pray the following prayer of thanksgiving with you; ask him or her to make the response "Lord, we thank you" at the proper time.

"Lord Jesus, you gave your life for us on the cross. Lord, we thank you. You became our Bread of Life. Lord, we thank you. You stay with us always. Lord, we thank you. Through you and with your Spirit, we share in a new and everlasting life. Lord, we thank you. Amen."

Singing If you wish, bring this home session to a close by singing with your child Song 8 on the record *We Celebrate the Eucharist*.

Reminder

Please sign your child's book on pages 51 and 55.

Storytelling   You might select a story from those recommended on page 92, above, and read it to your child during the week. Then help him or her relate it to what he or she has discovered in this lesson about sharing our life and love.

New Birth   Prepare with your child some "welcome" gift for a new baby expected in the family or neighborhood. Point up the fact that the new baby itself is a gift.

Tell your child about the phone calls (or whatever means you used) to tell the family about his or her expected birth.

Seeds and Seedlings   Plant some seeds with your child in a window box or some other container. Explain how the ancients thought seeds had to die in order to be reborn to new life, so that planting a seed is a symbol of Jesus' death and resurrection. Or tell your child about the caterpillar that becomes a butterfly.

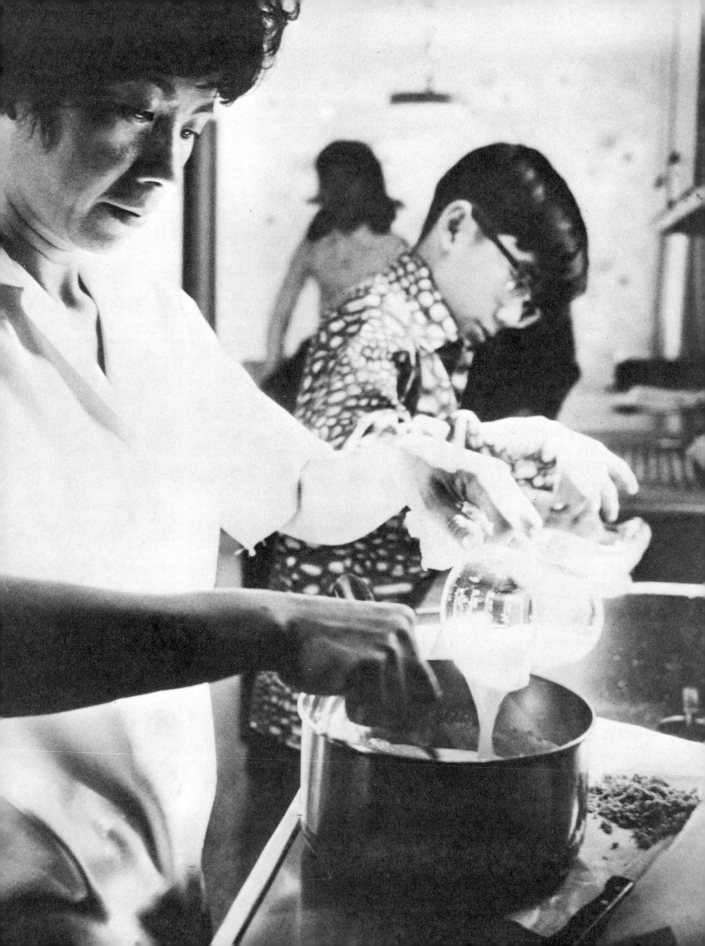

The Eucharist:

It's About Sharing a Meal

Eating and drinking are not merely necessities in our life, things we have to do simply to remain alive. They can and probably should be activities whose meanings extend beyond the purely useful or necessary. They are signs of companionship and unity, times for sharing interests and life.

Eating and drinking together seems always to have had this meaning. It was certainly so in the time of Jesus. We know this from looking at the celebration of the first Eucharist. Quite clearly, the first eucharistic celebration was a meal, a gathering of close friends to share food and drink for a purpose beyond the purely utilitarian.

The scriptural accounts of the celebration reveal the early Church's understanding of the meaning of that meal.

Whether or not the Last Supper was actually a Passover meal, it was certainly understood by the gospel writers to have been influenced by the atmosphere of the Passover week, during which it took place. The

Passover meal is described in the Old Testament as a memorial or commemoration. " 'This day shall be a memorial feast for you, which all your generations shall celebrate with pilgrimage to the Lord, as a perpetual institution' " (Exodus 12:14). The Israelites were to commemorate their liberation from slavery in Egypt—the event that sealed God's covenant with them.

At the same time, the meal was a covenant pledge for the future. Sharing food and drink at this meal was indeed a sign of the unity the Israelites experienced because of what God had done for them.

At the farewell supper he shared with his friends, Jesus took the core of a meal steeped in the tradition of the Passover—something clearly understandable to his disciples—and gave it a permanent and immensely richer meaning. He announced, through it, his death and resurrection. This new commemoration recalls God's new and most wonderful work for us—deliverance in Christ from sin and death. It renders Christ present to us through the mediation of the bread and wine we share.

Because this the Eucharist was clearly a meal, the sharing of food and drink was central. Thus it was a sign of the unity that the followers of Christ have. It was a source of the unity they share because, through sharing in the bread and wine, they share Christ. In our own Eucharist, although the meal as such has disappeared, sharing food remains central.

> *I am the bread of life. . . .*
> *I myself am the living bread*
> *come down from heaven.*
> *If anyone eats this bread*
> *he shall live forever;*
> *the bread I will give*
> *is my flesh, for the life of the world. . . .*
> *For my flesh is real food*
> *and my blood real drink.*
> *The man who feeds on my flesh*
> *and drinks my blood*
> *remains in me, and I in him (6:48, 51, 55-56).*

Saint John's choice of words is important. His understanding of the Eucharist centers around *nourishment and life.* The understandings of the other evangelists and of Saint Paul center around *life-giving sacrifice.*

We need the perspective offered by Saint John to appreciate the full significance of eating and drinking together in the Eucharist. Through his eyes we see that the food and drink we share in the Eucharist is true nourishment which has life-giving power.

It is in the Communion rite of the Eucharist that the gift offered is accepted. After we have declared our Yes to Christ who offers his life-giving presence to us, we pray together the Our Father, in which we ask God for the sustenance we need to live as his sons and daughters. Then we exchange a greeting of peace, a sign of oneness we have in Jesus and which we seek to strengthen in him.

Finally, the celebrant breaks the eucharistic bread for the community and invites us to come and share in this nourishment and its life-giving power. It is this Communion together that makes possible our personal communion with Jesus. Then this personal communion makes possible an even deeper union together, "one in Christ Jesus" (Galatians 3:28). After we have received Communion, the celebrant prays in our name, and his prayer frequently points to the sacramental Communion in which we have participated as a manner in which Jesus Christ draws us closer to himself and closer to one another.

Group Session

To help the children discover the meaning of bread and wine and the real communion that comes from the love that unites people at a meal

Aim

Welcome the children individually. Acknowledge the work they did on page 55 of their book.

Review

Show the children a few grains of wheat, a cup of flour, and a piece of bread. Discuss the process involved in making a loaf of bread from many grains of wheat. Describe how the wheat is grown, harvested, repeatedly ground and sifted, and formed into one bread. Reflect on the symbolic meaning of the bread: Many parts are gathered to become one. Bread can be broken into many pieces to nourish many people. It can be shared, and it gives the same strength to all.

Bread is made of many grains of wheat.

99

Wine is made of many grapes.

Show the children some grapes and a glass of wine. Discuss the process involved in making wine. Discuss how the grapes are grown, harvested, crushed, and how the juice is collected to become wine. Explain that many grapes are needed to make one cup of wine.

Explain that wine is a special beverage; it quenches thirst but it also gives joy. In many families, when special friends are invited to dinner, wine is served at the meal to show the joy of the occasion. In some places, when people want to show that they wish to live in peace with one another, they drink wine from the same cup, which they pass from one to another.

We share special meals with our family and friends.

Ask the children to name some times when their family shares a special meal together; for example, Thanksgiving Day, Christmas, a birthday, an anniversary. Help them reflect on what makes these meals special times. Discuss how everyone present gives something of himself or herself to make these meals occasions to share love and joy in their family.

Talk with the children about times they invite friends to their home to share a meal. Explain that when people invite others to share a meal they are saying, "We want you to consider yourself as part of our family. All that we have—our home, our food, our joy, our love—we share with you. Right now you are part of our family."

Activities

Picture Discussion Ask the children to open their book to pages 56 and 57. Encourage them to interpret the pictures. You might guide the discussion along the following lines: "Look at the girl in the first picture. Why, do you think, does she look so happy? Do you think this meal might be a special meal—perhaps Sunday dinner? What do you like best about Sunday dinner?

"The people in the next picture are Chinese. Notice the food on the table. Notice how they are sharing food from the same dishes. These people seem to be sharing their meal with friends. How can you tell there is more than one family at this meal?

"Look at the two boys in the next picture. How can you tell they are friends? When do you and your friends share snacks? When do snacks really taste the best?

"The mother in the last picture is preparing dinner. Who is helping her? Do you think the mother is glad to have someone help her? How

100

can you help your parents prepare a meal? Does your helping give joy to others? To whom especially?"

Reading Have the children turn to page 58. Read the text with them, or ask individuals to read a sentence each. Let them think for a few minutes about what they can do to help bring joy to their meals at home.

Writing Instruct the children to write in the space provided on page 58 ways in which they can bring joy to their meals at home.

Drawing Ask the children to describe by drawing or writing on page 59 what sharing a special meal with their family means to them. Encourage them to express the atmosphere that surrounds special meals.

Interpretation When a child has completed this work, ask him or her to tell you about it. Provide direction with specific comments; for example, "This certainly looks like a happy family. Who is this person? Who is this? Let me see if I can find you in the picture. Do these people share a meal with you every day? Why are they in the picture?"

Singing Teach the children a song that expresses the joy and love shared at a meal, such as Song 9 on the record *We Celebrate the Eucharist*. Teach also any songs that have been chosen for the First Communion celebration, such as Songs 12, 13, and 14 on the record. (These are the Communion songs that have been composed for the program.)

Celebration Have a small celebration. Ask the children to set up a special table with colorful tablecloth, flowers, and appropriate decorations. Provide a juice drink for the children. Together share a loaf of homemade bread or cake. Break off pieces and give one to each child.

Prayer Before sharing the food and drink, ask the children to listen attentively as you pray the following prayer of thanksgiving. "Lord Jesus, we thank you for the meals we share every day with our family and with those we love. We thank you for the joy of being together. We thank you for inviting us soon to Holy Communion.

Ask the children to respond to this prayer by singing the song taught in class.

Reminder
Attendance Records Fill in the attendance record and the cumulative record you are keeping on each child.

Complementary
Activities

☼ If time allows, prepare the children for the celebration for Theme 8 by using page 79 of *Celebrations*.

☼ Show a film or tell a story.

Films

Bread and Wine. TeleKETICS. 5 min., color.

Christmas in Denmark. Arthur Barr Productions. 10 min., color.

Christmas in Sweden. Films of the Nations. 14 min., color and b&w.

Books for Storytelling

Holdsworth, William Curtis. *Little Red Hen*. New York: Farrar, Straus & Giroux, 1969; $4.95.

Minarik, Else H. *Little Bear*. New York: Harper and Row, 1957; $3.79.

Zolotow, Charlotte. *When the Wind Stops*. Harper and Row, 1975; $4.50.

☼ Consider using some of the recommendations below for the home session.

Home Session

Aim

To teach your child how he or she will receive the Bread of Life

Review

The pictures on pages 56 and 57 of the "golden book" offer you an opportunity to speak with your child about gratitude for food and for people to share food with. You might also remark on the joy in sharing a meal, as the pictures show. Ask your child to show you the work he or she did on pages 58 and 59. If your child wishes to add to it, encourage this.

Jesus
shared meals
with his friends.

Explain to your child that Jesus, too, shared meals with his friends. The New Testament tells us that he was often invited to have dinner with Lazarus and his sisters, Mary and Martha, who were all Jesus' close friends.

Discuss another meal that Jesus shared with his friends: a wedding reception in Cana. Describe the setting, with its festivity, joy, and fellowship. Note that wine was served to the guests. Describe what Jesus did to save the bride and groom from embarrassment when the supply of wine had run out and to make the reception a thoroughly enjoyable feast.

Jesus invited his friends to share in a special meal. If your child attended the last celebration with you, he or she will be familiar with the atmosphere of the Last Supper. Review what Jesus did at the Last Supper. You might ask a few questions to help your child recall the details. "What do you remember about the Last Supper? Whom did Jesus invite to his meal? Do you remember what Jesus gave his friends to eat? What did they drink? What did Jesus do with the bread? What did he say? What did Jesus do with the cup of wine? What did he say?"

Point out Jesus' great love for his friends and his desire to remain with them always to share his life with them. You could read once more the account of the Last Supper on page 52 of your child's book.

Remind your child that he or she has learned a great many things since beginning to prepare for full participation in the Eucharist. He or she has learned how to behave in God's house, how to make peace with others, how to celebrate and sing with God's friends, how to listen to God's Word, how to give thanks to the Lord. He or she has also learned that the bread we receive at the meal of the Lord is the Bread of Life and that Jesus is really present with us in the Eucharist. Soon your child will be able to join with other members of God's family and receive Jesus, the Bread of Life.

The Communion Invitation Point out that during Mass, shortly before we receive Holy Communion, the priest invites us to share in the meal of the Lord. He says to us, "Happy are those who are called to his supper." Read with your child the text on page 60 of the "golden book." Help him or her learn the response, "Lord, I am not worthy...."

Liturgical Emphasis

The Communion Procession Recall with your child the people at Mass leaving their places at Communion time and going up to the celebrant to receive Holy Communion. Mention that as the people approach the celebrant, they sing a song to welcome Jesus, who gives himself to us. Sing together the song that has been selected in your parish for the First Holy Communion procession, or Song 12, 13, or 14 on the record *We Celebrate the Eucharist.* (These are the Communion songs that have been composed for the program.)

The Rite of Communion Ask your child to look at the picture on page 61. Stress the respect and the faith expressed by those who receive Holy Communion. Witness to your own faith in Jesus, the Bread of Life.

You might say, "When I am about to receive Holy Communion, I see a piece of bread but I believe that it is the Lord because Jesus says to me, 'I am the Bread of Life, and if you eat this bread you shall live forever.' The celebrant says to me, 'The Body of Christ.' I answer, 'Amen,' and this means 'Yes, Lord, I believe in you.' "

Reading Read together the text on page 62. Ask your child to think about how much he or she wishes to receive Jesus in Holy Communion.

Writing Have your child write or dictate to you a special prayer to Jesus. Space is provided for the prayer on page 62.

Gestures Show your child how we hold our hands and how we walk— slowly and reverently—when we go up to receive the Bread of Life. Demonstrate the manner in which you receive Holy Communion in your parish. The practice for receiving may vary from parish to parish and from diocese to diocese. It would be wise to tell your child that there are other ways of receiving, so that he or she will not be surprised to see other practices in another church.

Show your child the hosts you were given at the last celebration. Explain that they are pieces of bread. Give your child one of them so that he or she may discover how it tastes. Then give him or her a second one in the way it will be given in Holy Communion. Tell your child the person giving Communion says "The Body of Christ." Have your child practice answering "Amen" before receiving.

If Communion is to be received under both species, give your child a little wine to taste and show him or her how to hold the cup.

Explain how you as parents will approach the celebrant with your child, for you want to be *one* on this First Communion day. Tell him or her to remain for a moment with you until you have also received, and then to return to your place together.

Drawing Ask your child to turn to page 63 of the "golden book." Read the words at the top of the page and comment briefly on them. Then ask your child to show how you will all celebrate his or her First Holy Communion.

Reminder

Please sign your child's book on pages 59 and 63.

Storytelling You might read to your child one of the stories suggested on page 102, above, and then relate it to Theme 8.

Prayer At bedtime during the week you might pray together the prayer your child composed to tell Jesus how much he or she wishes to receive him in Holy Communion.

Invitations Make a list of people your child would like to invite to his or her First Holy Communion. Help your child write, decorate, and mail the invitations.

Baking Bread Bake some bread together. Call attention to the process whereby many grains of wheat have been crushed into flour. This reminded the early Christians of self-sacrifice. Then the flour becomes dough, so that the grains of wheat are now blended together into one loaf. This reminded the early Christians of our coming together into one as members of the one Jesus, members of his body, in loving self-sacrifice and in Holy Communion.

Sharing Bread and Wine Celebrate a simple family meal rite, using wine and home-baked bread. Help your child bake a loaf of bread. Let him or her carry the loaf of bread to the table whole, where it will be broken and shared. Place glasses on a tray and pour a little wine in each, unless a soft drink is preferred for the children under Communion age. The candidate for initiation into the Eucharist holds the loaf, while someone else prays as follows.

"God our Father, we offer you the bread that [Name] has made for us. Let it become a sign of our wish to live together in love, in peace and in oneness as your Son Jesus wants us to live."

Then one of the parents, or an older brother or sister, holds the tray with the glasses of wine and prays:

"God our Father, we offer you this wine, which we are going to share. Let it be a sign of the joy we have in living together. Let your Holy Spirit come into our hearts to teach us to share our joy. We ask this through Jesus Christ our Lord. Amen."

Then proceed with the meal, breaking and eating the bread as part of the meal. Talk quietly of the bread as a symbol of oneness and the wine as a symbol of gladness.

105

The Eucharist:

It's About Going Forth to Make a Better World

We spend a great deal of our life waiting, but all our waiting is not of the same quality or character. Sometimes we wait simply to accomplish some relatively insignificant but functional task. Sometimes we wait in order to do something or to have something done to us that we do not at all relish. But at times the waiting is more than mere waiting because it is a source of joy and happiness. Then our waiting becomes joyful anticipation.

Such is often the case when we look forward to the celebration of a special event in our life or in the life of someone in our family. In moments like these, our waiting truly has a share in the joy of what is awaited. We get ready; we prepare; we look forward. Indeed, half the joy is in the anticipation.

Waiting is a distinguishing mark of the Christian. As a matter of fact, Scripture more than once directs the followers of Christ to wait, to be watchful, to be prepared. And Scripture also clarifies the essential quality of Christian waiting. Because of what is awaited, our waiting turns to joyful anticipation.

INTRODUCTION TO THE THEME

In the gospels of Matthew, Mark, and Luke, what is awaited is the fulfillment of God's reign of love and peace that Christ came to inaugurate, the final realization of the kingdom of heaven or the kingdom of God.

The reign of God was already present in Jesus Christ. Asked by the Pharisees when the kingdom of God was to come, Jesus gave them this answer: "You cannot tell by careful watching when the reign of God will come. Neither is it a matter of reporting that it is 'here' or 'there.' The reign of God is already in your midst" (Luke 17: 20-21).

But that same reign had yet to spread through the whole world. That is the object of our waiting. And he told them a parable: "Notice the fig tree, or any other tree. You observe them when they are budding, and know for yourselves that summer is near. Likewise when you see all the things happening of which I speak, know that the reign of God is near" (Luke 21: 29-31).

In John's gospel (10: 10), the ministry that Christ already fulfills is described in somewhat different terms:

> *I came*
> *that they might have life*
> *and have it to the full.*

What is awaited is that time when all people will possess life to the full—eternal life (John 17: 1-3).

> *Father, the hour has come!*
> *Give glory to your Son*
> *that your Son may give glory to you,*
> *inasmuch as you have given him*
>   *authority over all mankind,*
> *that he may bestow eternal life on*
>   *those you gave him.*
> *(Eternal life is this:*
> *to know you, the only true God,*
> *and him whom you have sent, Jesus*
>   *Christ.)*

We Christians look forward to God's reign of love and peace, when all shall have life to the full and shall know the Lord. That day will be a day of great rejoicing, and its joy is something we already share in—in the waiting.

The same priestly prayer of Christ that describes the object of our waiting indicates what we are to be during that time of waiting, so that the ministry Christ began may touch every person. Jesus prayed (John 17:21),

> *that all may be one*
> *as you, Father, are in me, and I in you;*
> *I pray that they may be [one] in us,*
> *that the world may believe that you sent me.*

We Christians are meant to be a sign of extraordinary unity in this world.

This spirit of waiting, so characteristic of Christian life, colors the whole of Christian liturgical celebration. It is expressed at the core of the Eucharist itself in the Memorial Acclamation of the community, following the narration of the first Eucharist. "Christ has died. Christ is risen. Christ will come again."

That proclamation reminds us of Saint Paul's declaration to the Christian community at Corinth: "Every time, then, you eat this bread and drink this cup, you proclaim the death of the Lord until he comes!" (1 Corinthians 11:26).

Not only is the spirit of waiting itself expressed in the liturgy, but also how we are to prepare for what we await. It is particularly the dismissal that summarizes what we are to do during this time of waiting. This important rite is brief, and unfortunately it often goes practically unnoticed.

It begins with the salutation to and blessing of the community by the priest. This act recalls the opening of the eucharistic celebration itself, and through it we know that the same God who invited us to this celebration, and was thereby present among us, is still with us as we go forth.

Then the priest charges the community to "Go in peace to love and serve the Lord." He sends us forth as faithful servants of the Lord to build up his kingdom, to bring to fulfillment his own reign of peace and love. He commissions us to spread the joy that has characterized our waiting to everyone we meet and to every situation we enter. Our response and our closing song express our intention to fulfill our mission.

109

They show our desire to hasten the day when it can truly be said, "...and he shall be their God who is always with them. He shall wipe every tear from their eyes, and there shall be no more death or mourning..." (Revelation 21:3-4).

Group Session

Aim

To help the children discover how they can make this world a better place in which to live and thus prepare for a better world to come

Review

Greet all the children with special joy. Ask them to tell you about their First Holy Communion and to describe the happiness of the occasion. Have them show you their drawing on page 63 of their "golden book" and any pictures of their First Holy Communion that they might have brought to class.

This is the world in which we live.

Display pictures of beautiful things, happy situations, and joyful people. Explain to the children that in the world there are many beautiful people and beautiful things. A great many people share their life and love with us. They care for us and bring us happiness. Consider the many admirable qualities in people and the positive aspects of the world.

Display pictures of unhappy situations and people. Explain to the children that everything in the world is not all beautiful and happy. There are both joy and sadness in the world, health and sickness, peace and war, friendship and quarreling, riches and poverty, beauty and ugliness. Ask the children to name conditions shown in the pictures that militate against the presence of beauty, joy, and happiness in this world.

We want to make a better world for all.

Ask the children to think about what they can do to make their own neighborhood a better place in which to live, their own school a better place in which to learn, people they meet every day happier. Consider with them the many ordinary, everyday ways by which people can enrich the world and other people.

Picture Discussion Ask the children to open their book to pages 64 and 65. Encourage discussion of the pictures in the light of what has just been considered in class. You may wish to use the following as a guide.

"Look at the children in the first picture. Where do you think they are rushing? What do you suppose they are planning to do? What are some things you do with your friends that you really enjoy doing?

"The girl in the second picture has such a happy face. Wouldn't the world be a better place if everyone had a smiling face? What can we do to help people have smiling faces?

"The children in the next picture are playing violins in a concert. They are developing their talents. They are playing music for people to listen to and enjoy. Think of the marvelous things we can do. How can we bring joy to others?

"What are the children in the last picture doing? How are they making their neighborhood a better place? How are they helping others? Look at what is painted on the wall. Love is their message to everyone in their neighborhood."

Reading Ask several children to read a paragraph each on page 66 of their book. Reflect with them on specific ways in which their family, teachers, neighbors, and friends show love for them.

Writing Ask the children to fill in the spaces on page 66. Help those who may have difficulty with writing.

Drawing Read to the children the words found at the top of page 67. Then ask them to express how they can show their love for others. Some children might prefer to write a story or paste pictures cut from magazines.

Interpretation As each child finishes this work, invite him or her to show it to you and tell you about it. Be specific in helping the children express their thoughts. You might say, "Tell me about this person. Why did you choose him (her) for your picture? Who is *this* person? How does this person bring joy to the world? How do you feel knowing that you can show your love to all these people?"

Singing Teach the children Song 10 or Song 11 (or both) on the record *We Celebrate the Eucharist.* Song 10 emphasizes our own contribution to a better world, while Song 11, "Come, Lord Jesus," stresses the gratuity of God's gift, through Jesus, of the better world we are preparing. Both songs are appropriate for this theme.

Prayer Close the session with the following prayer. Ask the children to repeat each petition after you. "Lord, send us forth to share your Spirit of joy in our family. Lord, send us forth to spread your Spirit of peace in our neighborhood. Lord, send us forth to show your love to people."

Reminders

Attendance Records After the session, fill in the attendance record and the cumulative record you are keeping on each child.

Certificates Fill out and sign each child's Communion certificate. Add a personal note. A suitable format appears just inside the front cover of the "golden book." Assist in the implementation of whatever plan the program director has for having this certificate (or another instead) properly completed. Encourage each child to write, in a spirit of quiet celebration, the names of the "people present to celebrate," just inside the back cover of the child's book.

Complementary Activities

⚙ Show a film or tell a story.

Films

In Touch with God. TeleKETICS. 3 min., color.

Martin the Cobbler. Billy Budd Films. 28 min., color. (This new film, recognized as one of the finest of its genre ever produced, is simply Tolstoy's story "Where Love is, God is" in animated clay. The Russian author interprets Matthew 25:40—"As often as you did it for one of my least brothers, you did it for me"—in a most appealing and altogether authentic fashion.)

Swimmy. Connecticut Films. 6 min., color.

Talent for Tony. St. Francis Productions. 12 min., color.

Books for Storytelling

Estes, Eleanor. *The Hundred Dresses.* New York: Harcourt Brace Jovanovich, 1974; $1.50.

Harris, Rosemary. *The Child in the Bamboo Grove.* New York: S. G. Phillips, 1971; $5.95.

Hill, Elizabeth Starr. *Evan's Corner.* New York: Holt, Rinehart & Winston, 1967; $5.95.

Lionni, Leo. *Frederick*. New York: Pantheon, 1966; $5.99.
————. *Swimmy*. New York: Pantheon, 1963; $5.99.
Merrill, Joan. *Maria's House*. New York: Atheneum, 1975; $4.95.
Prather, Ray. *New Neighbors*. New York: McGraw-Hill, 1975; $4.95.

✿ Consider using some of the activities suggested below for the home session.

Home Session

To foster faith and hope in the coming of a better world, and to give your child a deeper awareness of his or her Christian commitment to people and to the world

Aim

Ask your child to consider how people make his or her life happy and how he or she can share this joy and happiness with others. You might use the pictures on pages 64 and 65 of the "golden book" to aid in your discussion. Referring to the first two pictures, you might ask your child to reflect on what brings happiness. Using the other two pictures, you might consider together ways in which your child can use his or her own special gifts and talents to bring joy to other people.

Review

Describe to your child the world God has promised us—a world in which we shall live in peace, joy, and happiness. It will be a world without wars, sickness, quarreling, tears, or death. It will never end. You might read from your New Testament, or describe in your own words, Chapter 25, verses 31-45, of the Gospel of Saint Matthew.

God promises us a better world.

Point out to your child that there are many ways in which people can renew the present world and thus prepare for the better world that God promises us. You are aware, more than anyone else, of some of the practical and realistic ways in which your child can personally bring more joy, more friendship, more happiness, more beauty to the world. Awakening a child to respond creatively and confidently to the world around us is most effectively fostered within the family.

We can prepare for a better world.

Liturgical Emphasis

Our Mission Explain that during the moments of silence after Communion, we thank God for all his gifts and ask Jesus to give us his Spirit of love to help us discover ways in which we can bring more joy and peace to the world—at home, in school, and in our neighborhood.

The Blessing Point out that shortly before we leave God's house, the celebrant blesses us. He prays that we may love and serve the Lord every day. Read page 68 of the "golden book" with your child. Then you might reread the words of the celebrant and ask your child to give the responses.

The Recessional Encourage your child to describe how people leave God's house. "Why do we sing? What thoughts are in our hearts?" Ask your child to describe what the picture on page 69 says to him or her. Help him or her to integrate what you have discussed together with what the picture is saying about going forth to make a better world. The Spirit of love, the friendship, and the joy evident in this picture might serve as guides.

Activities

Singing Sing together Song 10 or Song 11 on the record *We Celebrate the Eucharist.*

Reading Summarize Theme 9 by reading pages 70 and 71 of the "golden book" with your child. Then consider together ways in which he or she can daily personalize Jesus' words so that they do not remain abstract concepts but become a way of life. Turn to pages 72 and 73. Reflect on the picture, and witness to your own faith and hope in the better world that God promises us.

Review

Page through all nine themes in the "golden book," helping your child summarize how "we celebrate the Eucharist" together in the house of God. As you go through the themes, you could also sing the songs for each theme on the record.

Prayer Conclude this session with an adaptation of the Prayer of Saint Francis. Pray each sentence and ask your child to repeat it after you. "Lord, make us your helpers in this world. Where there is sadness, help us bring joy. Where there is hatred, help us bring love. Where there is quarreling, help us bring peace."

114

Reminder

Sign your child's Communion certificate. Add a personal note.

Storytelling You might read to your child one of the stories suggested on pages 112–113, to complement what has been considered in this theme.

Poster Study the life of a missionary (Albert Schweitzer, or Father Damien the Leper, for example), and make a poster to illustrate what he or she did to make a better world.

Questions Study together the questions and answers in the back of your child's book, and relate them to the nine themes of WE CELEBRATE THE EUCHARIST.

Meditation Meditate together the texts on pages 70 and 71 of the "golden book" in the following manner. Read a short paragraph together; then ask yourselves in silence, before the Lord, what it might mean for your daily life, for your life tomorrow. "What can I do soon? And what can I do one day?" Then, in the same spirit of quiet in the presence of Jesus, exchange with your child your plans to make God's world better at home, in the neighborhood, and in the outside world. At the end of your meditation, choose one particular and definite thing to do, and then, afterward, do it together.

NOTES

NOTES

NOTES

NOTES

NOTES

NOTES

NOTES

2 3 4 5 6 7 8 9 10 PP 83 82 81 80 79 78